GRAY
MATTER

Cells of the
Nervous System

GRAY
MATTER

GRAY
MATTER

Cells of the Nervous System

Jennifer R. Morgan and Ona Bloom

CHELSEA HOUSE
PUBLISHERS
A Haights Cross Communications ✦ Company ®
Philadelphia

CHELSEA HOUSE PUBLISHERS

VP, NEW PRODUCT DEVELOPMENT Sally Cheney
DIRECTOR OF PRODUCTION Kim Shinners
CREATIVE MANAGER Takeshi Takahashi
MANUFACTURING MANAGER Diann Grasse
PRODUCTION EDITOR Noelle Nardone
PHOTO EDITOR Sarah Bloom

STAFF FOR CELLS OF THE NERVOUS SYSTEM

PROJECT MANAGEMENT Dovetail Content Solutions
DEVELOPMENTAL EDITOR Carol Field
PROJECT MANAGER Pat Mrozek
ART DIRECTOR Carol Bleistine
SERIES AND COVER DESIGNER Terry Mallon
LAYOUT Maryland Composition Company, Inc.

A Haights Cross Communications ✦ Company ®

www.chelseahouse.com

First Printing

10 9 8 7 6 5 4 3 2 1

Library of Congress Cataloging-in-Publication Data

Bloom, Ona.
    Cells of the nervous system / Ona Bloom and Jennifer Morgan.
    p. cm. — (Gray Matter)
Includes bibliographical references and index.
    ISBN 0-7910-8512-0
1. Neurons. 2. Neuroglia. I. Morgan, Jennifer, 1955– II. Title. III. Series.
QP361.B58 2005
611´.0188—dc22   2005011690

Contents

1 Introduction to the Nervous System

Think for a moment about some of your normal daily activities at school—running to class, memorizing the answer to a test question, calculating a mathematical equation, speaking to your classmates, or listening to your teacher's presentation. Then, think about how many times a day you feel emotions, dream, move your muscles, smell, see, hear, taste, or touch something. All of these actions require the use of your **nervous system**, which is the major system of control, regulation, and communication in the body. The nervous system consists of the brain, spinal cord, and complex networks of nerves that connect the brain and spinal cord to all parts of the body (Figure 1.1). The brain is at the center of all mental processes, including feeling emotions, planning, reasoning, and learning. The spinal cord and nerves mainly transmit information about sensation and body movements to and from the brain.

The nervous system can be divided into three functional systems with distinct roles: the sensory, motor, and associational systems. The **sensory systems** acquire and process information about the environment. They are the "input" systems in the body. Sensory systems include those that process information about the five senses: sight, sound, taste, smell, and touch. The **motor systems** respond to the information taken in by the sensory systems. They are the "output" systems in the

(A)

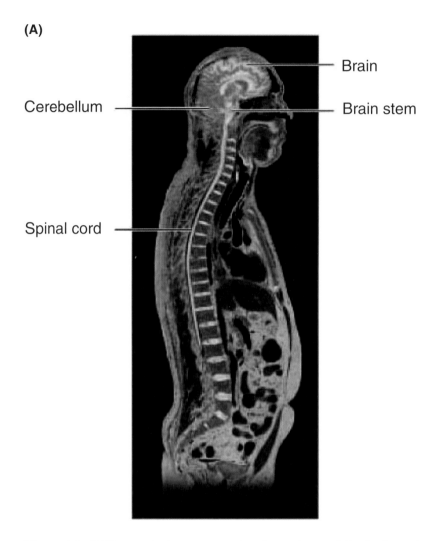

Figure 1.1 **(A)** The central nervous system is made up of the brain and spinal cord. Also shown here are the cerebellum and brain stem, two major parts of the brain.

body. Motor systems are those that control voluntary skeletal muscle movements. The **associational systems** work between the sensory and motor systems by processing the "input" information and setting up "output" responses. Associational systems also process higher brain functions, such as language, learning,

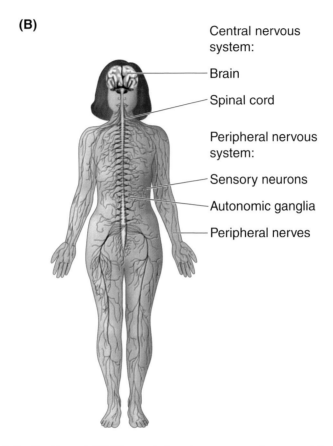

(B)

Central nervous system:

Brain

Spinal cord

Peripheral nervous system:

Sensory neurons

Autonomic ganglia

Peripheral nerves

Figure 1.1 *Continued.* **(B)** The peripheral nervous system consists of an elaborate network of nerves that reach all body parts.

planning, and reasoning. Each of these systems—the sensory, motor, and associational systems—includes elaborate nerve circuits that transmit information to and from the brain, as well as internal circuits within the brain. The systems all work together to ensure that the body can perceive the internal and external environment and then respond appropriately.

A BRIEF HISTORY: STUDYING THE NERVOUS SYSTEM

The brain is often thought of as the most important part of the nervous system because of its capacity to perform complex mental processes. The first known reference to the brain was made in 1700 B.C., in an ancient Egyptian document called a papyrus. This document is thought to have been written by the great physician Imhotep, who was also the architect of the first Egyptian pyramid. In 1862, the papyrus was acquired by an American named Edwin Smith. When Smith died, his daughter gave the papyrus to the New York Historical Society. Nobody knew the meaning of the document until 1920, when the Historical Society hired Dr. James Henry Breasted to translate the Egyptian hieroglyphs on the papyrus into English. Dr. Breasted found that the papyrus included 27 reports of head injuries. Surprisingly, Dr. Breasted found that the papyrus contained the first detailed description of the brain and spinal cord. From this document, which is now called the Edwin Smith Surgical Papyrus, we learned that the ancient Egyptians realized that damage to the brain and spinal cord was often irreversible. However, the ancient Egyptians did not place much value on the brain. When someone died, for example, they removed the brain by pulverizing it and draining it out through the nose, and they threw it away before mummifying the body. In contrast, the heart and other organs were carefully preserved and buried along with the body.

Over time, the importance of the brain for communication and for body regulation became clear. However, as recently as 120 years ago, nobody knew what substance made up the brain and spinal cord. It took an intellectual battle between two European scientists during the late 19th century to uncover the composition of the nervous system. Italian scientist Camillo Golgi thought the nervous system was composed of a continuous, unbroken web of material called a reticulum. In contrast, Spanish scientist Santiago Ramón y Cajal thought that the nervous system was made up of many individual cells that were separate from each other (Figure 1.2). To find the answer, Ramón y Cajal used a special dye that was designed by Golgi to

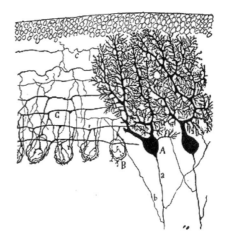

Figure 1.2 *(Left)* Santiago Ramón y Cajal won the Nobel Prize in Physiology or Medicine for discovering that the basic unit of the nervous system is the neuron. *(Right)* This drawing is one of his illustrations showing several kinds of neurons.

stain various parts of the brain. He then took the brain samples, examined them with a microscope, and sketched what he saw in a series of elaborate pictures. Using this approach, Ramón y Cajal demonstrated clearly in 1887 that the brain was indeed made up of individual brain cells called **neurons**. For their important work on the structure of the nervous system, Ramón y Cajal and Golgi won the Nobel Prize in Physiology or Medicine in 1906.

Now we know that the human nervous system is made up of billions of neurons and even more of their supporting cells, which are called **glia**, or neuroglia. This book focuses on the neurons and glia, their roles in the developing and adult nervous systems, and how they respond to injuries, diseases, and drugs.

THE ANATOMY OF THE NERVOUS SYSTEM

To begin, let us first learn some anatomy of the nervous system. The nervous system can be divided into two main parts: the

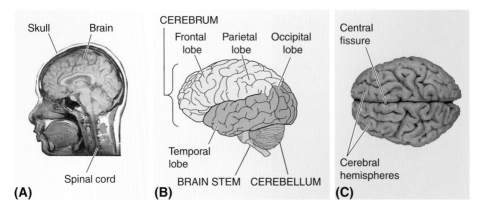

Figure 1.3 Several views of the brain. **(A)** An MRI image showing fine details of the nervous system. **(B)** A diagram showing a side view of the human brain. **(C)** A view from the top of a human brain showing the cerebrum.

central nervous system (**CNS**) and the **peripheral nervous system** (**PNS**) (refer again to Figure 1.1). The central nervous system consists of the brain and spinal cord. The peripheral nervous system consists of an elaborate network of nerves that reaches out to all parts of the body. Together, the CNS and PNS acquire and process information from the environment, plan how the body will react to this information, and carry out the appropriate responses.

The Central Nervous System

The brain, the center of mental activity for the nervous system, is encased and heavily protected by the skull (Figure 1.3A). The average adult human brain weighs about 3 pounds (1,400 grams), which is about 2% of your total body weight, and contains around 100 billion neurons. The parts of the brain that can be seen on the surface are the cerebrum, the cerebellum, and the brain stem (Figure 1.3B).

The **cerebrum** (also called the **forebrain**) is the largest part of the human brain. It is divided into two symmetrical halves called **cerebral hemispheres**, which are separated by a prominent crevice called the **central fissure** (Figure 1.3C). The right cerebral hemisphere is almost entirely separate from the left one, except for a thick nerve bundle connecting the two halves deep within the middle of the brain. In general, the right cerebral hemisphere controls the left side of the body and the left cerebral hemisphere controls the right side of the body. Most brain functions require cross-talk between the two cerebral hemispheres. However, in some cases, only one cerebral hemisphere dominates certain brain functions. For example, the left cerebral hemisphere controls language processing (see "Right Brain Versus Left Brain" box).

The outer portion of the cerebrum is highly folded and is called the "cortex." If the adult human cortex were flattened out, it would cover an area the size of a full sheet of newspaper. Each cerebral hemisphere is divided into four functionally different regions, called lobes (refer back to Figure 1.3B). The **frontal lobe** is involved in reasoning, planning, organization, emotions, and problem-solving. The frontal lobe is also the site of working memory, a type of short-term memory that stores information that is being used for only a few seconds. For example, you are using working memory right now to remember what the first half of this sentence said as you read the end of the sentence (see "A Case for the Frontal Lobe: The Story of Phineas Gage" box). The **parietal lobe** is located behind the frontal lobe and processes sensory information from the environment. For example, the parietal lobe processes incoming information from the body's surface, including information about touch to the skin. The **temporal lobe** is located below the parietal lobe and the lateral fissure. It is mainly concerned with processing auditory (hearing) information. The **occipital lobe** (from *oculus*, the Latin word for "eye") is located at the back of the brain. This region processes many aspects of visual information. There are also many more structures underneath the cerebral hemispheres that lie deep within the brain. These structures process information about memories, emotions, and sleep, among other things. As you can see, the cerebrum is responsible for many complex and specialized brain functions.

Behind the cerebrum, at the back of the brain, is the **cerebellum.** The cerebellum controls many aspects of voluntary movement. It helps the body plan and coordinate complex, precise, fine movements. For example, the cerebellum controls lip and tongue movements while speaking, leg and arm movements while running, or finger movements while playing a musical instrument. The cerebellum also helps you maintain balance. It receives inputs from the cerebrum, which are concerned with the

Right Brain Versus Left Brain

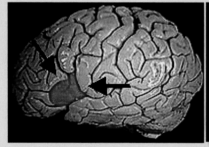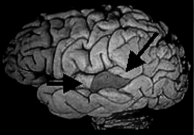

Broca's area (red) and Wernicke's area (blue) deal with language production and comprehension.

Not all brain functions are equally directed by both sides of the brain. Instead, one cerebral hemisphere may dominate when performing a particular task. This phenomenon of one-sided domination is referred to as "lateralization." One of the best examples of a lateralized brain function is the process of language, which occurs on the left side of the brain in 95% of people. The language areas of the brain were discovered in the late

planning of movements. The internal circuits of the cerebellum then process the information and send outputs back to the parts of the cerebrum concerned with initiating and making the appropriate movement. In this way, the cerebellum helps minimize errors, allowing the body to make smooth and highly coordinated movements. Not surprisingly, people with injuries to the cerebellum often move in a stiff, jerky, and uncoordinated manner.

Underneath the cerebellum and cerebrum is the **brain stem**. The brain stem is a relay station that transmits sensory and motor information between the brain and spinal cord. It also processes information going to and coming from the head and the

1800s by two European doctors, Karl Wernicke and Paul Broca. Broca found that patients with damage to one part of the left frontal lobe could not produce language. While these patients could not speak, they had no problem understanding language. In contrast, Wernicke found that patients with damage to another part of the left cerebral hemisphere could not understand language, but could produce speech. However, these patients made no sense because they jumbled up their words. Taken together, these studies showed that distinct and specific regions of the left cerebral hemisphere control language production or comprehension. These regions are now called Broca's area and Wernicke's area. Damage to the same regions of the right cerebral hemisphere does not interfere with language, emphasizing the point that language is lateralized to the left hemisphere. In addition to language, many other brain functions are at least partially lateralized. For example, the left half of the brain is dominant when processing math and logic. The right half of the brain is dominant when using spatial abilities, recognizing faces, and processing visual images.

neck. Furthermore, the brain stem regulates some aspects of consciousness, i.e., the mental state of being self-aware.

Besides the brain, the other major part of the central nervous system is the **spinal cord**, which begins at the base of the brain stem and runs the entire length of the upper body. It is encased in and heavily protected by the bones of the spine, which are called vertebrae. The spinal cord has several important jobs related to the generation of body movements. In particular, the spinal cord sends out nerves (bundles of neuron extensions) that connect to skeletal muscles all over the body. These nerves drive the contraction and relaxation of skeletal muscles during walking, running,

A Case for the Frontal Lobe: The Story of Phineas Gage

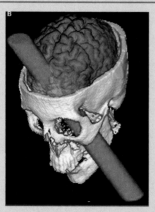

This illustration is a computer reconstruction of Phineas Gage's injury.

Phineas Gage was a foreman for a railroad construction crew in the 1940s. His team had been hired to lay down tracks for a railroad line going to Burlington, Vermont. One day, while clearing the land for the tracks, an accidental explosion drove a tamping iron through Gage's head. The iron was 3 feet, 7 inches long; weighed 13.5 pounds; and was 1.25 inches in diameter on its thickest end. It entered under Gage's left cheekbone and exited from the top of his head, landing 25 to 30 yards away. Although the accident destroyed most of the front left side of his brain, Gage miraculously recovered enough to leave the hospital after only 10 weeks. Months later, he re-

swimming, and all other voluntary movements. The spinal cord also contains the sensory nerve endings that receive information from the skin about temperature, pressure, and pain. If a harmful stimulus is detected, such as touching the sharp point of a thumbtack, the spinal cord then initiates the appropriate muscle movements needed to retreat from the offending stimulus. Interestingly, the generation of patterned movements, such as walking and running, is driven entirely by the spinal cord itself. However, inputs to the spinal cord from the brain can slightly alter muscle movements. For example, inputs from the cerebellum help create smooth movements.

sumed work at the railroad contracting company, but he was not the same. Before the accident, Gage had been a reliable worker, a good businessman, and an efficient foreman. After the accident, Gage became unreliable, irresponsible, and often lashed out in impatience. His intellectual skills were preserved, but his friends said that he was "no longer Gage." Years later, after he died, Gage's body was exhumed so that his brain injury could be studied more carefully. Several scientists used X rays and computer models to analyze the extent of the damage. This analysis revealed severe damage to the frontal lobe of Gage's brain. Scientists Hanna and Antonio Damasio and their coworkers have examined many other patients with frontal lobe damage. Like Gage, these patients can remember facts and calculate mathematical equations, but they have a hard time maintaining commitments, relationships, and jobs. Therefore, the frontal lobe may control some important aspects of personality. Using this approach, the Damasios have examined more than 1,500 patients with various brain injuries to try to determine the relationship between the brain and behavior.

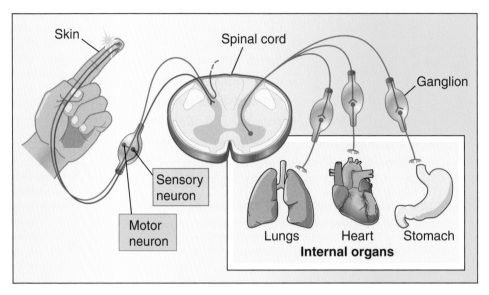

Figure 1.4 The peripheral nervous system is made up of collections of sensory and motor neurons that reside in small sacs called ganglia. These neurons receive and process information from the skin and control smooth muscle contractions of internal organs.

The Peripheral Nervous System

The peripheral nervous system (PNS) is made up of elaborate networks of nerves that extend to all parts of the body (recall Figure 1.1). The neurons of the PNS are distinct from those of the central nervous system because they are clustered together within small sacks that lie along both sides, but outside, of the spinal cord. These sacks of neurons are called **ganglia** (singular is *ganglion*) (Figure 1.4). Mainly, the PNS processes sensory and motor information between the spinal cord, the skin, and the internal organs. Accordingly, the ganglia of the PNS contain two main types of neurons: sensory and motor neurons. The **sensory neurons** detect heat, pain, and pressure through receptors on the skin, and send that information to the spinal cord. The **motor neurons** connect to internal smooth muscle organs, such as the lungs, heart, and stomach, and control their contractions. In this way, the PNS also controls the body's response to stressful situations. For example, if you suddenly encountered a large, angry dog, the PNS would increase your rate of breathing and your heartbeat while slowing down digestion in order to prepare you for a rapid response to the stress. In this way, the PNS helps the body decide whether to stay and fight or run away, a reaction called the "fight or flight" response.

The remainder of this book focuses on the cells that make up the central and peripheral nervous system—the neurons and glia. The goal of the book is to discover how neurons and glia control the body's actions and reactions. You will discover how these cells build the brain and spinal cord and connect to the rest of the body during development. You will also learn how these cells process information about sight, smell, hearing, taste, and touch. Furthermore, you will learn about the radical changes in the nervous system that continue to occur into adulthood, including how neurons and glia respond to injury. Finally, the book discusses how diseases and drugs of addiction can harm the cells of the nervous system. In this way, you will receive an overview of the nervous system from the standpoint of the neurons and glia from which it is made. As you will see, although the cells of the nervous system are small, they perform some of the largest roles in the entire body.

■ **Learn more about the nervous system** Search the Internet for *central nervous system* or *peripheral nervous system*.

2 Neurons: The Brain's High-Speed Internet

All tissues, organs, and systems of the body are made of huge collections of individual **cells**, the basic units of life. Within the nervous system, the brain, spinal cord, and peripheral nerves are made from elaborate networks containing billions of nerve cells called neurons. There are many different types of neurons, and each type has a different shape, size, and role in the brain and spinal cord (Figure 2.1). Together, these neurons encode, transmit, and store information about everything from your thoughts and senses to your body movements, dreams, and memories. The human brain contains about 100 billion neurons—a number so large that if you counted 1 neuron per second, it would take 3,171 years to count all the neurons in your brain. If you flattened all the neurons in your brain, the total surface area would cover four soccer fields. Given all the complex jobs of the nervous system, perhaps it is not surprising that there are so many neurons in your nervous system to cover all that mental ground. Amazingly, neurons can transmit information through the brain at speeds up to 220 miles per hour—about the cruising speed of a small, twin-engine airplane.

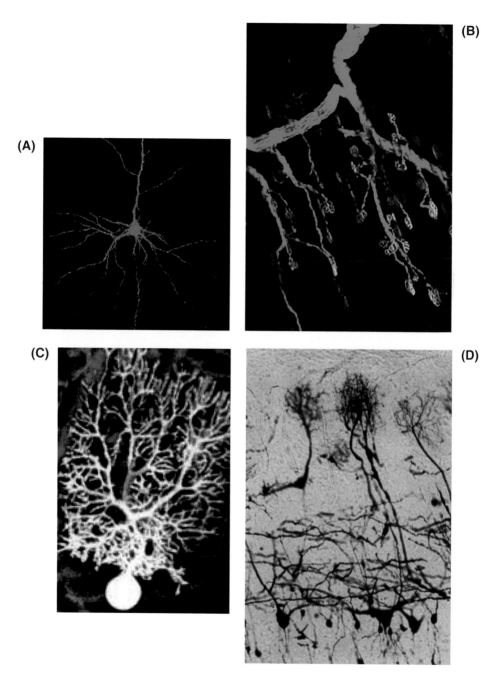

Figure 2.1 Neurons come in many shapes and sizes. These neurons are from **(A)** the mouse brain cortex, **(B)** the peripheral nervous system, **(C)** the cerebellum, and **(D)** the olfactory bulb (smell center). (Colors are due to dyes or indicators.)

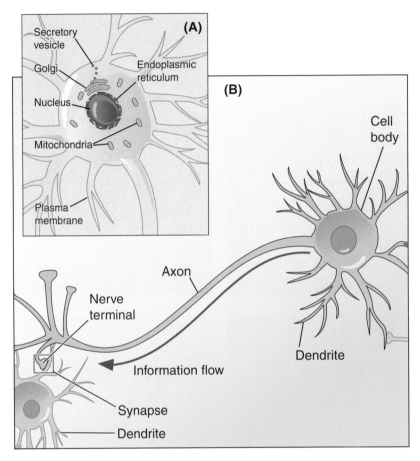

Figure 2.2 (A) Neurons contain smaller internal cellular compartments, called organelles, which include the nucleus, endoplasmic reticulum, Golgi apparatus, secretory vesicles, and mitochondria. **(B)** Neurons have two different ends—a receiving end (the dendrites) and a transmitting end (the nerve terminal). The synapse (red box at lower left) is the site of communication between two neurons.

HOW NEURONS ARE LIKE OTHER CELLS OF THE BODY

Although diverse in shape and function, neurons share some similarities with other cells in the body. For example, like cells of the skin, kidney and intestines, neurons are encased by a **plasma membrane** at the cell surface (Figure 2.2A). Neurons also contain smaller internal cellular compartments, called **organelles**, which include the nucleus, endoplasmic reticulum, **Golgi apparatus**, secretory vesicles, and mitochondria. The **nucleus** holds the genetic material, which is called **deoxyribonucleic acid** (**DNA**). The **endoplasmic reticulum** (ER) is a complex network of membranes extending from the nucleus that helps the cell synthesize **proteins** (polymers of amino acids strung together). The Golgi apparatus modifies and packages proteins into **secretory vesicles** so that they can be delivered to the cell surface for secretion. **Mitochondria** make **adenosine triphosphate** (**ATP**) and therefore provide the energy for these processes in all cells, including the neurons. Together, these organelles control many processes that are essential to the function and survival of the neurons.

Despite all the similarities with other cells in the body, neurons are also unique, because they do not readily divide. If a neuron dies, in most cases it cannot be regenerated. This explains why you are born with more neurons than you will have later in life. Furthermore, this explains why recovery from brain and spinal cord injuries—such as those seen with head trauma, stroke, drug abuse, and disease—is more difficult than recovery from injuries to other body systems. Neuron regeneration does occur sometimes and will be discussed in Chapters 5 and 7. Some scientists believe that neuronal **stem cells** may be a potential source of replacement neurons. Remember, neurons are precious. Treat them well.

ANATOMY OF A NEURON

Another distinguishing feature of neurons is their complex, irregular shape. Neurons have two different ends—a receiving end and a transmitting end. Each end carries out a specialized set of roles for the cell (Figure 2.2B). One end of the neuron receives incoming information "from" other neurons. The other end of the neuron transmits information "to" other neurons. At the receiving end are structures called **dendrites**, which are small projections that extend from the neuron like branches extend from a tree. In fact, the word *dendrite* is derived from *dendros,* the Greek word for "tree." Dendrites receive information from other neurons. This information is then carried to the **cell body** (also called the "soma") of the neuron. The cell body integrates all the incoming information. A single projection extends from the cell body, and is called an **axon**. Like an electrical cable, the axon transmits information very rapidly from one end of the neuron to the other. The longest axon in the body is the one that extends from the base of the spine to the big toe. In the average adult human, this axon is 3 feet (1 meter) long. In a giraffe, this same axon is 15 feet (4.6 meters) long. At the ends of axons are small swellings called nerve endings, or **nerve terminals**. Nerve terminals contact neighboring neurons and transfer information to them. As you can see, each part of the neuron has a special role in allowing communication to occur throughout the nervous system (see "Making Neurons Glow with Green Fluorescence" box).

Within the mature nervous system, cell bodies, dendrites, and nerve terminals are grouped together (Figure 2.3). Because of their grayish tint, the layers of the CNS containing these structures are collectively called **gray matter**. Likewise, axons are grouped together. Because axons are coated with a white, fatty substance called **myelin**, the layers containing these structures are called **white matter** (for more on myelin, see Chapter 3).

THE SYNAPSE

The contacts between nerve terminals of one neuron and other neurons are called **synapses** (Figures 2.2 and 2.4), a term that was coined in 1897 by Charles Sherrington. The word *synapse* was derived from the Greek words *syn,* which means "together," and *haptein,* which means "to clasp" or "to hold." So, the synapse is the place where two neurons are held together and through which information is transferred from one neuron

Making Neurons Glow With Green Fluorescence

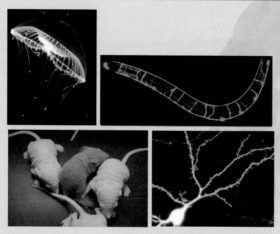

GFP originates from a jellyfish (*top left*) and can be used to study neurons in a variety of other animals such as the worm (*top right*) and the mouse neuron (*bottom right*). GFP can also be used to study other cell types, such as the skin cells, as is shown by the green mice (*bottom left*).

Neuroscientists are scientists who study the nervous system. They often want to observe the sizes, shapes, and movements of a living neuron in order to understand how neurons work. Past approaches required killing neurons through chemical fixation, allowing only a single snapshot of a neuron. However, in 1994, Martin Chalfie, a scientist at Columbia University, revolutionized our ability to visualize living neurons in action. Chalfie coaxed neurons from a worm to produce a green fluorescent protein (GFP), which is normally found in the Northwest Pacific jellyfish, *Aequorea victoria*. To do so, he transferred the DNA encoding for jellyfish GFP into the DNA of worm neurons. When the neurons produced GFP, they glowed bright green and could be observed through a microscope. Because GFP is harmless to neurons, the neurons can be kept alive and studied over a long period. In other words, scientists can observe dynamic changes in the neuron by making movies of the glowing neurons. GFP has now been used to study single neurons in culture as well as neurons within a whole brain. It has also been used to study many other cell types in the body. Furthermore, fluorescent proteins of different colors—red, yellow, and blue—can be used in combination with GFP to study several cellular processes at once.

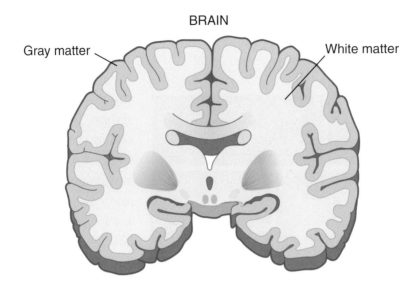

BRAIN

Gray matter

White matter

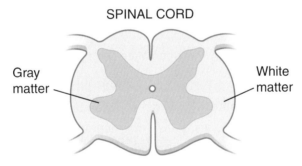

SPINAL CORD

Gray
matter

White
matter

Figure 2.3 The layers of the brain and spinal cord that include cell bodies, dendrites, and nerve terminals are collectively called "gray matter." The layers containing axons and myelin are called "white matter."

to another. Thus, the synapse is the communication station of the neuron. Each of the 100 billion neurons in the nervous system forms between 100 and 1,000 synapses with other neurons. Therefore, the brain has between 10 trillion and 100 trillion (between 10^{13} and 10^{14}) synapses, through which a nearly endless supply of information is transmitted.

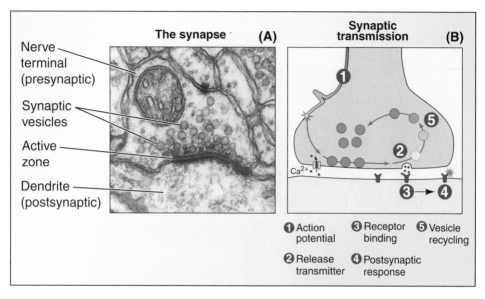

Figure 2.4 **(A)** The synapse is the site where neurons communicate with their targets (other neurons, muscles, or organs). **(B)** Synaptic transmission is the process by which neurons communicate.

Most synapses in the brain and spinal cord are **chemical synapses**, meaning that chemical molecules serve as the messenger between neurons. There are also **electrical synapses**, where electrical impulses serve as the messenger between the neurons. Because chemical synapses are the most common, we will focus on these. Chemical synapses occur between the nerve terminals of one neuron and the dendrites, cell body, axons, or nerve terminals of another neuron. However, not all chemical synapses are between two neurons. For example, in the peripheral nervous system, some neurons form chemical synapses with internal organs, such as the heart, lungs, and stomach (recall Figure 1.4). Furthermore, there are many chemical synapses in which neurons contact muscles, which are called **neuromuscular junctions**. At each synapse, the "sending" side is referred to as **presynaptic** (Figure 2.4A). The "receiving" side is referred to as **postsynaptic**.

At chemical synapses, neurons communicate with each other through a process called **synaptic transmission** (Figure 2.4B). Critical for synaptic transmission are special secretory compartments in the nerve terminal, called **synaptic vesicles** (Figure 2.4A). There are several hundred synaptic vesicles clustered within each nerve terminal, and each of them is filled with

Spiders, Snakes, and Snails: Makers of Harmful Neurotoxins

The black widow (*left*) and the cone snail (*right*) produce neurotoxins that dramatically affect the process of synaptic transmission.

Some spiders and snails—along with many other animals in nature—produce harmful substances that selectively attack the nervous system. These substances are called neurotoxins. Normally, neurotoxins are used by the animal for protection or for capturing prey. However, a person unfortunate enough to be exposed to a neurotoxin through a sting or a bite can also experience the harmful effects, which may include paralysis, irregular heartbeat and breathing, and sometimes even death.

Many neurotoxins produce their harmful effects by altering the process of synaptic transmission. For example, latrotoxin, the neurotoxin in black widow spider venom, causes massive neurotransmitter release at neuromuscular junctions, inducing severe muscle contractions. As a result, a person bitten by a black widow often has painful muscle cramps and difficulty breathing. Alpha-bungarotoxin, which is found in the venom of

chemical molecules called **neurotransmitters** (see "Spiders, Snakes, and Snails: Makers of Harmful Neurotoxins" box). Synaptic vesicles are clustered around a special region of the nerve terminal membrane called the **active zone** (Figure 2.4A). Synaptic transmission begins when the appropriate signal—an all-or-none wave of electrical excitation called an **action potential**—

cobras, blocks neurotransmitter receptors at the neuromuscular synapses. Therefore, a person bitten by a cobra may experience severe muscle paralysis. Conotoxins, the neurotoxins found in the venom of the marine cone snail, prevent action potentials or neurotransmitter release or block neurotransmitter receptors. A sting from the cone snail results in pain, numbness, paralysis, and sometimes death.

These are just a few of the 100 neurotoxins that exist in nature. Neurotoxins are made by a variety of bacteria, fungi, plants, and animals. Though they are scary substances, neurotoxins can also be beneficial in a controlled environment. For example, scientists use neurotoxins as tools in the laboratory to block synaptic transmission as a way to learn more about this process. Medical doctors use the bacterial botulinum neurotoxin (Botox®) to treat patients with abnormal muscle spasms. Because Botox causes muscle relaxation, it alleviates the pain that comes with muscle spasms. Although the Food and Drug Administration (FDA) has also approved Botox for the cosmetic purpose of reducing frown lines, it is often used incorrectly to reduce other facial wrinkles. This misuse may put patients at risk for unwanted muscle weakness. Although neurotoxins have some beneficial medical uses and even though some antivenoms are available, you should still be careful not to approach any potentially dangerous creatures when swimming or exploring.

reaches the nerve terminal (Figure 2.4B). The action potential triggers one, or possibly several, synaptic vesicles to fuse with the presynaptic plasma membrane and release the neurotransmitter contents. The neurotransmitter molecules diffuse across a very small gap between the presynaptic and postsynaptic neurons, which is called the **synaptic cleft**. Once the neurotransmitters reach the postsynaptic neuron, they bind and activate special neurotransmitter receptors on the cell surface. Activation of the neurotransmitter receptors generates a response in the postsynaptic neuron, and the communication transfer between the neurons is complete. Synaptic transmission is so fast that there is only about 1 millisecond ($1/1,000^{th}$ of a second) between the arrival of the action potential in the nerve terminal and the postsynaptic response. Fast synaptic transmission occurs every time you move, and every time that you taste, smell, see, hear, and touch something. Every thought, memory, and behavior you have is the result of complex patterns of synaptic transmission between neurons (refer back to "Spiders, Snakes, and Snails: Makers of Harmful Neurotoxins" box).

With each event of synaptic transmission, a synaptic vesicle is lost from the cluster due to its fusion with the plasma membrane. Without a way to replenish the synaptic vesicles, the nerve terminal would quickly become empty of vesicles and neurotransmitters, and communication between the neurons would shut down. To prevent this from happening, nerve terminals recycle their synaptic vesicles by recapturing them from the plasma membrane (Figure 2.4B). Next, the newly recaptured vesicles are refilled with neurotransmitter molecules and shuttled back to the cluster, where they can be used for another round of synaptic transmission. In addition to recycling synaptic vesicles, the nerve terminal also recycles the neurotransmitter molecules from the synaptic cleft. To do so, neurotransmitter molecules are taken from the synaptic cleft back into the presynaptic nerve terminal via special shuttling molecules called **neurotransmitter transporters**. By efficiently recycling synaptic vesicles and neurotransmitter molecules, the nerve terminal can continue its communication with neighboring neurons over a long period of time.

NEUROTRANSMITTERS AND THEIR RECEPTORS

In order to achieve its complex functions, the nervous system uses many different chemicals as neurotransmitters. In fact, more than 100 known chemical compounds are considered neurotransmitters. In general, nerve terminals make and secrete only a single neurotransmitter (although there are some exceptions). Neurotransmitters are grouped into two types: **excitatory** and **inhibitory**. Excitatory neurotransmitters "excite," or increase the activity of the postsynaptic neurons that detect them. Inhibitory neurotransmitters "inhibit," or decrease the activity of the neurons that detect them. Most neurotransmitters are excitatory. The major excitatory neurotransmitter is called **glutamate** . Because more than half of the synapses in the brain and spinal cord use glutamate as a neurotransmitter, it is generally considered the most important neurotransmitter in the central nervous system. The major inhibitory neurotransmitter is called **GABA**, which stands for *gamma-amino*butyric *a*cid. **Acetylcholine**, or ACh, is another excitatory neurotransmitter that is used in the peripheral nervous system and causes muscle contractions. ACh is also used in regions of the brain that control movements and memory. Other interesting excitatory neurotransmitters are **serotonin, dopamine**, and **norepinephrine**. Serotonin regulates sleep, wakefulness, states of alertness, and emotions. Dopamine is involved in motivation and reward. Perhaps for this reason, some drugs of addiction, such as cocaine and nicotine, affect brain pathways that use dopamine. Dopamine is also found in a few brain regions that coordinate body move-

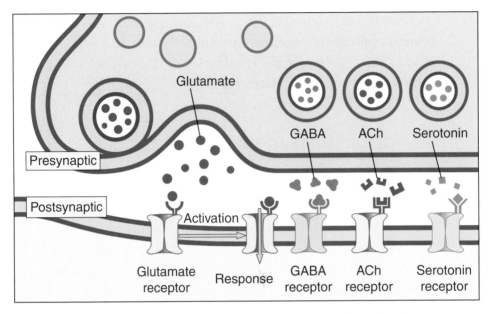

Figure 2.5 There are many kinds of neurotransmitters. Binding of each neurotransmitter (glutamate in this case) to its appropriate receptor triggers a response in the postsynaptic cell.

ments. Parkinson's disease specifically attacks these regions, causing individuals affected by this disease to have tremors and uncoordinated movements. Norepinephrine is a neurotransmitter that is a derivative of dopamine. Together with other neurotransmitters, it helps regulate the body's "fight or flight" response to stress. Many medications that successfully treat anxiety disorders, depression, and schizophrenia target pathways in the brain that use either serotonin or norepinephrine or both. The relationships between diseases, drugs, and neurotransmitters are discussed in more detail in Chapters 8 and 9.

Each neurotransmitter is detected by specific receptors on the postsynaptic cell surface (Figure 2.5). For example, glutamate is detected by glutamate receptors, while GABA is detected by GABA receptors. Detection of neurotransmitters is like a lock-

and-key mechanism; the receptor is the lock and the neurotransmitter is the key. As long as the correct match is made, the postsynaptic neuron will be activated and information will pass across the synapse. During development of the nervous system, neurons with the correct lock-and-key combination wire up together. This pairing ensures effective neuronal communication. Sometimes, neurotransmitter receptors are also sensitive to other compounds in addition to the appropriate neurotransmitters. For example, one class of ACh receptors responds to nicotine, an active ingredient in cigarette smoke. Therefore, these receptors are called nicotinic ACh receptors. Another class of ACh receptors responds to an active compound found in some wild mushrooms called muscarine. These receptors are called muscarinic ACh receptors. Compounds like nicotine and muscarine, which activate receptors by mimicking neurotransmitters, are called **agonists**. In contrast, other compounds called **antagonists** block the neurotransmitter receptors and prevent them from responding to the appropriate neurotransmitters.

Now you have all the basic tools for understanding what neurons are and how they communicate with each other. In the next chapter, you will learn about the other major class of cells in the nervous system, the glial cells, and how they interact with neurons.

■ **Learn more about neurons** Search the Internet for *neurons*, *synapse*, or *neurotransmitters*.

3 Glia: More Than a Supporting Role

Albert Einstein was one of the most famous mathematicians and physicists of the 20th century. Many people consider him a genius. Because of his incredible intelligence, several researchers over the years have wondered whether there was something different about Einstein's brain. When Einstein died in 1955, Thomas Harvey, the pathologist who performed the autopsy, quickly removed the brain and preserved it in his laboratory at Princeton. As a result, several researchers gained the opportunity to examine the structure of Einstein's brain in some detail. In the 1980s, Marian Diamond, one such researcher, became interested in examining the areas of Einstein's brain where complex brain functions occur. So, Diamond began her hunt for Einstein's brain. She soon discovered that Thomas Harvey had moved to Missouri, and he had taken the brain with him. She tracked down Harvey and asked him if he would provide her with a small sample that she could examine under her microscope. Three years later, Marian Diamond finally received a package with four sugar cube–sized samples of Einstein's brain. She and her colleagues cut the brain samples into very thin slices and examined them under the microscope. When she did this, Diamond discovered that certain regions of Einstein's brain contained almost twice the number of glia, the non-neuronal supporting brain cells, compared to the number found in the average adult human male. In contrast, the number of neurons in Einstein's brain was normal. Interestingly, the largest increase in the number of glia was found in the association cortex, a region where complex brain functions such as attention, analysis, and planning occur. Although there was only one such brain to examine, Marian Diamond's study suggests that glial cells may influence a person's ability to perform these higher order brain functions.

■ **Learn more about Einstein's brain** Search the Internet for *Einstein*, *brain*, and *glia*.

Glial cells are non-neuronal, dividing cells found in both the central and peripheral nervous systems (see "How the Brain Grows" box). Named for the Greek word for "glue," glial cells provide structural support and nutrients to neurons.

How the Brain Grows

At birth, your brain contains nearly all the neurons it will ever have and weighs approximately 400 grams (0.882 pounds). However, your brain continues to grow. By the time you reach adulthood, your brain will weigh between 1,300 and 1,400 grams (between 2.9 and 3.1 pounds)—more than three times what it weighed when you were born. Because neurons do not divide, it is initially perplexing to understand how the brain grows. The answer to this mystery is found in the glial cells of the brain. Glial cells continue to divide and grow throughout your life, resulting in an increase in the overall size of the brain. A bigger mystery is exactly what keeps the glial cells from overmultiplying. When this unlikely event occurs, a cancerous brain tumor is formed. Therefore, many treatments for brain cancer are aimed at preventing glial cells from overmultiplying.

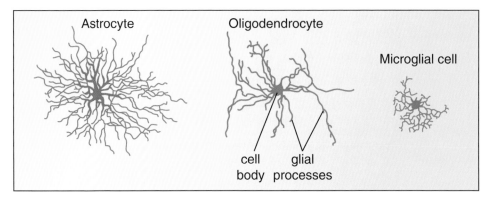

Figure 3.1 The major types of glia in the central nervous system are called astrocytes, oligodendrocytes, and microglia.

Glial cells are incapable of producing the action potentials that are used by neurons for rapid communication. Instead, to pass on and receive information to other glial cells or neurons, glia slowly release and detect other chemical signals. The major types of glia in the nervous system are called **astrocytes**, **oligodendrocytes**, **Schwann cells**, and **microglia** (Figure 3.1). In addition to having different shapes, each type of glia has a unique set of functions in the brain.

Although there are approximately 10 times more glial cells in the brain than there are neurons, much less is known about glia. For a long time, researchers believed that glia existed in the brain only to provide structural and nutritional support for neurons. While it is true that glia support neurons, many recent studies over the past 20 years, including Marian Diamond's study on Einstein's brain, suggest that glia perform more complex and diverse roles in the nervous system than was originally thought.

ASTROCYTES: CELLS WITH MANY JOBS IN THE NERVOUS SYSTEM

Astrocytes are the largest and most abundant glial cells in the central nervous system. Their name, from the Greek word for "star"

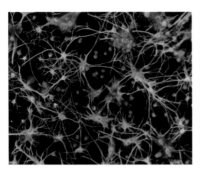 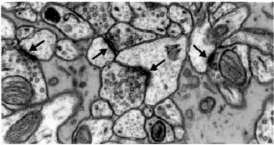

Figure 3.2 *(Left)* The image shows astrocytes (green) that are marked with a fluorescent dye. Notice the branch-like extensions that project away from the cell body. *(Right)* These extensions (blue) wrap tightly around the synaptic boutons *(arrows)*.

(*astro*), is due to their star-like shape (Figure 3.2). Astrocytes are found throughout the brain, interspersed between neurons, other glia, and blood-carrying capillaries. The branch-like extensions of astrocytes often wrap tightly around nerve terminals (Figure 3.2). Astrocytes communicate with neurons through close physical contacts with the synapses of the neurons. Like all other types of glia, astrocytes were once thought to provide only structural and nutritional support to neurons. However, new studies over the past 10 years have revealed that astrocytes also affect the development and activity of neurons. Therefore, astrocytes perform much more than a maintenance role in the brain.

Astrocytes Provide Nutrients to Neurons
One primary role of astrocytes in the brain is to supply neurons with the nutrients they need to stay alive and active. To do this, astrocytes pick up nutrients from blood vessels and shuttle them to the neurons (Figure 3.3). Critical for this process are special contacts that astrocytes make with a type of cell found in the brain's blood vessels—the endothelial cells (see "The Blood-Brain Barrier: Stopping Brain Invaders" box). Each special contact is called an endfoot. Astrocytic endfeet take up small

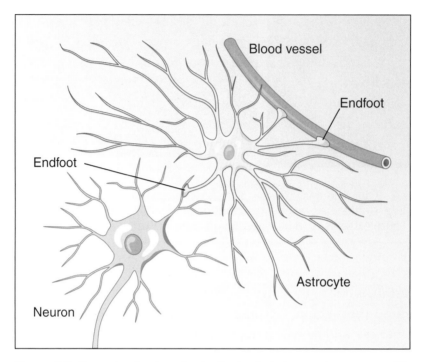

Figure 3.3 One role of astrocytes in the brain is to supply neurons with the nutrients they need to stay alive and active. To do this, astrocytes pick up the nutrients from the blood vessels with special contacts called endfeet and shuttle them to the neurons.

molecules, such as sugar (glucose), ions, and water, which pass through the endothelial cells (see Figure 3.3). Then, astrocytes transport and deliver the molecules to the neuron. Therefore, astrocytes are the pipelines between blood vessels and neurons.

Astrocytes Influence Synapse Development

Recent studies have revealed that astrocytes also have a remarkable influence on the number of synapses formed by a neuron during development. Soon after a neuron is born, it grows out a single axon that branches near its end and forms anywhere from 100 to 1,000 synapses with other neurons (see Chapter 4). Such plentiful synapse formation ensures that all the parts of the brain

The Blood-Brain Barrier: Stopping Brain Invaders

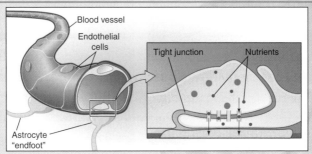

In the 19th century, scientist **Paul Ehrlich** discovered that colored dyes, when injected into the bloodstream, would stain all of the organs of an animal except for the brain. Later, his student, **Edwin Goldmann**, discovered that, if the dye was injected into the spinal cord, only the brain and spinal cord took the dye. These experiments revealed that there is a special barrier between the circulatory system and the brain, which we now call the *blood-brain barrier*.

The blood-brain barrier exists because of special endothelial cells that line the blood vessels in the brain. The blood-brain barrier forms a selective filter that protects the brain from foreign substances and helps maintain a stable environment. Therefore, the only substances that escape the endothelial cells are small molecules that can pass directly through their membranes, such as sugar, ions, and water. Larger molecules—including many drugs, antibodies, and hormones—cannot pass through. Certain conditions may cause the blood-brain barrier to break down temporarily, including high blood pressure, brain injury, and radiation. When this happens, the brain becomes unusually vulnerable to invasion by foreign substances. However, it is often difficult to treat brain infections by typical methods because most antibiotics will not cross the blood-brain barrier. Therefore, one major focus of brain research is to discover new drugs and new drug delivery methods so that brain infections might be more easily treated in the future.

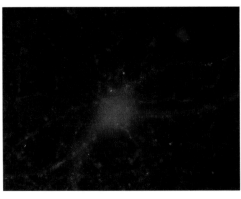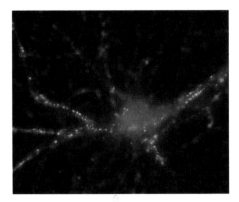

Figure 3.4 These photos show examples of neurons grown either without *(left)* or with *(right)* astrocytes. The small red dots are the synapses.

get connected. Studies performed in 2001 by Ben Barres and his colleagues at Stanford University showed that the presence of astrocytes is very important for this process of synapse formation. When Barres and his colleagues grew neurons in a culture dish in the absence of astrocytes, the neurons developed only a few, sparse synapses (Figure 3.4). Not surprisingly, these sparsely connected neurons also exhibited very little activity. In contrast, when the neurons were grown in the presence of astrocytes, the neurons formed six to seven times more synapses and were much more active. This study showed that astrocytes play an important role in the growth and activity of developing neurons.

Astrocytes Influence the Activity of Neurons

Astrocytes also influence the activity of mature neurons in several ways. One way is by controlling the amount of neurotransmitter available at the synapse. Following neurotransmitter release, astrocytes soak up the excess neurotransmitter from the synaptic cleft (Figure 3.5, left pathway). This rapid removal of neurotransmitter ensures that the postsynaptic neuron does not become overexcited, which could be deadly to the neuron. Once

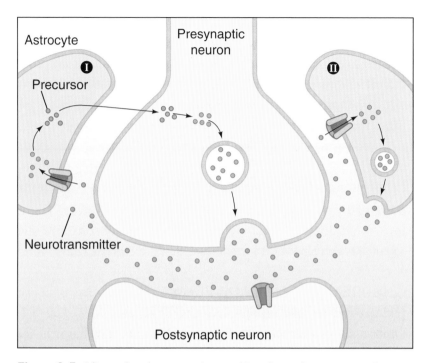

Figure 3.5 After releasing neurotransmitter from the presynaptic neuron, astrocytes soak up the excess through special transporters (purple), degrade it, and ship its precursor back to the neuron, where it is reused (I). Alternatively, the neurotransmitter is released from the astrocyte back onto the neuron where it can be detected by receptors (green; II).

inside the astrocyte, the excess neurotransmitter is degraded into its precursor, which is a substance from which another substance is made. The precursor molecules are then released by the astrocyte onto the neuron, where they are taken up and remade into neurotransmitter molecules. The neurotransmitters are then repackaged into synaptic vesicles and reused in another round of neurotransmitter release. By recycling neurotransmitter molecules, the astrocytes help neurons maintain an appropriate level of activity.

In addition to breaking down neurotransmitters into their pre-cursors, astrocytes may also repackage the neurotransmitters and release them back onto the neuron (Figure 3.5, right pathway). Al-though neurotransmitter release from astrocytes may utilize a similar mechanism to that which occurs at neuronal synapses, it is more than 100 times slower. Neurotransmitter released from as-trocytes can be detected by the postsynaptic neuron and some-times results in long-lasting changes in neuronal activity.

Finally, neurotransmitter released by astrocytes can also be detected by other astrocytes, both nearby and far away. There-fore, in addition to influencing neighboring neurons and glia, astrocytes can also send long-range signals to other cells.

OLIGODENDROCYTES AND SCHWANN CELLS: INSULATING THE NERVOUS SYSTEM

Other types of glial cells in the brain and spinal cord have the job of insulating neurons. In the central nervous system, these glial cells are called oligodendrocytes. In the peripheral nervous system, they are the Schwann cells. Both oligodendrocytes and Schwann cells send out very thin branches that wrap around the axons of neurons many times (Figure 3.6). This wrapping is rich in a fatty substance called myelin, and the process of wrapping is called "myelination." Because myelin is so fatty, it gives the white matter of the brain its color. (Gray matter is made of the dendrites, cell bodies, and nerve terminals of neurons.) The role played by myelin is similar to that of insulation on an electrical wire. The axon is the "wire." Myelin is the "insulation." The myelin insulation allows the axons to conduct nerve impulses (action potentials) very quickly and over long distances. Without myelination, the nerve impulse would leak out and grow fatigued a short distance down the axon, and the signal would never reach the next nerve terminal. Myeli-nation by oligodendrocytes and Schwann cells is essential for neu-ronal communication and for brain function.

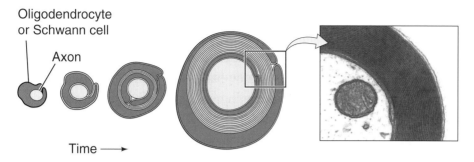

Figure 3.6 Oligodendrocytes and Schwann cells provide insulation to neurons by wrapping tightly many times around an axon.

Many diseases destroy myelin in either the central or peripheral nervous system. Destruction of myelin is called **demyelination**. Demyelination is thought to be the result of an abnormal autoimmune response in which the body starts to attack its own myelin. Why this happens is unclear. However, demyelination leaves bare spots on the axon (like a chewed piece of wire) through which the nerve impulse leaks out. When the nerve impulse leaks out, communication lines between neurons are broken. One common disease of demyelination, multiple sclerosis (MS), currently affects an estimated 2.5 million adults and children around the world. Multiple sclerosis will be discussed further in Chapter 8.

MICROGLIA: THE IMMUNE CELLS OF THE NERVOUS SYSTEM

Microglia represent yet another class of glia in the nervous system. As their name implies, microglia are among the smallest of all glial cells in the nervous system. They serve as the immune system for the nervous system by rapidly destroying invading microbes or removing dead cells in the brain and spinal cord.

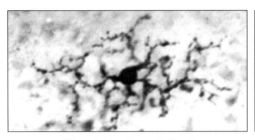

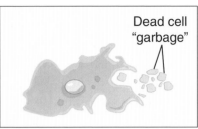

"Resting" microglial cell   "Activated" microglial cell

Figure 3.7 *(Left)* A microglial cell, shown here in its "resting state." *(Right)* Microglial cells in their "activated state" travel to sites of injury and "eat up" all the dead cells to prevent them from doing more damage.

Following nerve injury, trauma, stroke, or inflammation, microglia digest and clear dead neurons, a process similar to taking out the brain's garbage.

Unlike the other types of glial cells, which remain relatively stationary in the brain, microglial cells move around the brain as they respond to foreign invaders or dying cells. At rest, microglia have many branches, like a tree, and are interspersed between neurons (Figure 3.7). However, when microglia are responding to an invading microbe or dying cell, they change their shape to fit the brain terrain through which they must travel to reach the site of danger. If the microglia must move through spaces between neuronal cell bodies, they become rounded. However, if the microglia must move through spaces between axons, they may adopt a rod-like shape to squeeze between the long, cable-like processes. Once microglia reach the site of danger, they become rounder in shape and begin to **phagocytose**, or "chew up," the dead cell debris.

In addition to clearing dead neurons and invading microbes, microglia also produce and secrete several chemical compounds. In the developing brain, microglia secrete growth factors that might help the neurons grow axons and dendrites. In the mature brain, activated microglia secrete signaling messenger molecules. These molecules travel freely in the brain and may communicate signals to other neurons and glial cells. However, if overproduced, these substances can also harm healthy neurons. For example, overproduction of one type of signaling molecule produced by microglia, the cytokines, has recently been linked to several neurological diseases, including Alzheimer's and Parkinson's diseases. Therefore, it is important to understand what causes the microglia to overproduce signaling molecules, and to try to prevent this from happening.

This diverse array of glial functions indicates that these cells should no longer be considered simply the glue of the nervous system. After all, glial cells must be doing something very special if they outnumber neurons in the brain by 10 to 1.

4 Nervous System Development: Making and Breaking Connections

From the very moment of conception, the human body follows an elaborate developmental program that forms the head, the torso, the limbs, and the internal organs. Included in this developmental program are the processes that create the brain and the spinal cord (Figure 4.1). First, neurons and glia are generated. Then, the neurons are wired together and connected via synapses. During this process, many more connections are made than are necessary in order to ensure that each neuron receives proper input. The final step in the development of the nervous system is to remove the unwanted connections. To give you an idea of the magnitude of this important task, more than 100 billion neurons and a trillion glial cells are made during the 40 weeks between conception and birth. If that is not impressive enough, the neurons are connected together via trillions of synapses during this time. For all of this to occur reliably requires complex patterns of gene expression, cell-to-cell communication, neuronal migration, axon outgrowth, and synaptic rearrangements. This chapter highlights some of these amazing processes that occur during nervous system development.

EARLY NERVOUS SYSTEM DEVELOPMENT

Before the nervous system is formed, the embryo must progress through several critical stages of development. First,

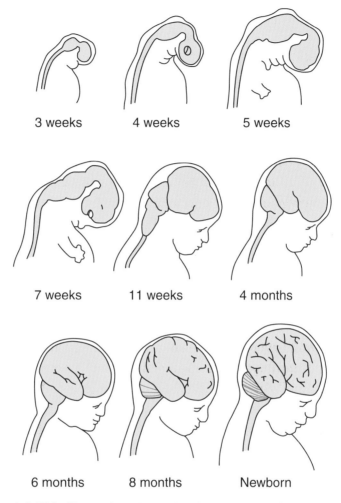

Figure 4.1 This illustration shows the development of the fetal brain from three weeks after conception through birth.

3 weeks   4 weeks   5 weeks

7 weeks   11 weeks   4 months

6 months   8 months   Newborn

fertilization of the egg by a sperm creates a cell with the appropriate content of genetic material from the mother and father. Once these components merge, cell division begins and the embryo starts to grow. The first step in the formation of the nervous system is the generation of nervous tissue that will later give rise to the neurons and glial cells. Nervous tissue is generated during

Gastrulation

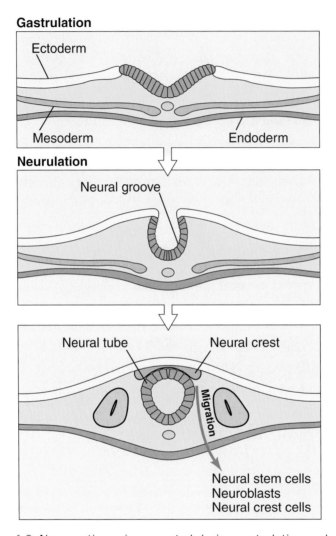

Figure 4.2 Nervous tissue is generated during gastrulation and neurulation, during which the embryonic neural plate is formed, transformed into the neural groove, and then into the neural tube. Migration of neuronal precursors from the neural tube is an important event in this development.

processes called **gastrulation** and **neurulation** (Figure 4.2). Gastrulation occurs first. During this process, the developing embryo undergoes an elaborate series of infoldings that generate three layers of cells. The outer layer of cells, called the **ectoderm**, is the layer from which the nervous system will be constructed. The middle layer of cells is the mesoderm (*meso* means "middle"), and the inner layer of cells is the endoderm (*endo* means "inner"). During gastrulation, midline body symmetry and front-to-back body asymmetry are also established. Next, neurulation occurs. During neurulation, the middle portion of the ectoderm thickens and folds inward to form the **neural groove** (see Figure 4.2). In the meantime, the embryo continues to grow longer. Finally, the ectodermal tube closes by zippering up. The zippering starts in the middle of the body and then proceeds in both directions to the ends. The final result is the formation of the **neural tube**, from which the brain and spinal cord will be generated (see Figure 4.2). A special region of the neural tube called the neural crest secretes substances that turn on special sets of genes, which establish the orientation of the nervous system. During this process, the boundaries are established that separate the forebrain (cerebrum), midbrain (brain stem), hindbrain (brain stem and cerebellum), and spinal cord.

When something goes wrong during neurulation, the consequences can be dramatic. For example, failure of the neural tube to close results in a condition called **spina bifida** (*bifida* means "split"), which affects 3,000 births each year in the United States. At birth, a baby with spina bifida has an underdeveloped spinal cord and often has a completely open lower back. Although spina bifida is a major developmental defect, it is not always lethal, as the neural tube can sometimes be closed with surgery. People affected by spina bifida often experience hydrocephaly (water on the brain), paralysis, and learning disorders. However, they can still lead fairly normal lives. About 70,000 Americans are currently living with spina bifida. Another disorder of neurulation occurs when the neural tube does not close on one end. This can result in the formation of an embryo without a forebrain. This rare condition is called **anencephaly** (meaning "no brain"), and it usually results in death within a few weeks after birth. Finally, mutations in genes that regulate the early formation of the brain can cause diseases of mental retardation, such as fragile-X syndrome, autism, and Down syndrome.

MAKING NEURONS

When the neural tube closes, **neurogenesis**, or "birth of neurons," begins from the neural tube. The neural tube contains three types of neural precursors, which give rise to all neurons and glial cells (see Figure 4.2). One type of precursor is the **neural stem cell** (see "Stem Cells" box). Neural stem cells divide to produce more precursor cells. These remarkable cells also have the capacity to become either a neuron or a glial cell. The second type of precursor cell is the **neuroblast**. Neuroblasts are nondividing and eventually give rise to neurons. The third type of precursor cell is the **neural crest cell**. Neural crest cells migrate out of the neural tube and then become either a neuron or a glial cell of the peripheral nervous system. Initially, all precursor cells are located in the innermost region of the neural tube. Here, the neural stem cells undergo many rounds of multiplication by cell division. At some point, they stop dividing and become neuroblasts. At the peak of neurogenesis, 250,000 new neurons are born each minute. Many more neurons are produced than are actually used in the final construction of the brain. The unused neurons are eliminated through a process called **apoptosis**, or programmed cell death (for more details about apoptosis, see Chapter 7).

■ **Learn more about stem cells** Search the Internet for *stem cells*.

After their generation, neuroblasts migrate from the neural crest to their final destination. As they migrate, neuroblasts sense signals from the local environment that dictate which type of neuron they will become (see Figure 2.1 for some good examples).

Stem Cells

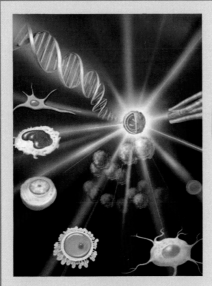

Stem cells are amazing because they can become any other type of cell in the body, including neurons. They might offer powerful tools for curing diseases of the nervous system in the future.

Stem cells are remarkable cells that have the amazing ability to become any other type of cell in the body. When a stem cell divides, each of the daughter cells can either remain a stem cell or can turn into another kind of cell with a more specialized function. For example, stem cells become cells of the brain, liver, heart, bone, or blood. Therefore, stem cells offer the exciting potential to treat injuries and diseases that affect many parts of the body, including the nervous system. For example, stem cells might be used in the future to replenish the neurons that die as a consequence of Parkinson's or Alzheimer's diseases, spinal cord injury, stroke, heart disease, diabetes, and burns (see Chapters 7 and 8). Stem cells are derived from embryonic (fetal) tissues or from adult tissues and can be grown in culture in a laboratory. Embryonic stem cells seem to be more flexible than adult stem cells, meaning that they can turn into more kinds of cells than adult stem cells can. Thus, embryonic stem cells offer the best choice for developing treatments for diseases and injuries. However, the use of embryonic cells is currently very limited in the United States due to ethical, political, and religious concerns.

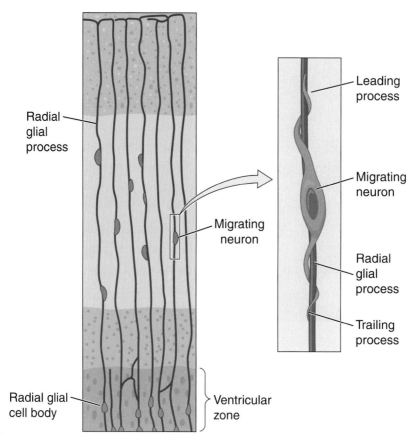

Radial
glial
process

Radial glial
cell body

Migrating
neuron

Ventricular
zone

Leading
process

Migrating
neuron

Radial
glial
process

Trailing
process

Figure 4.3 Neuroblasts use radial glial cells to migrate to their final destination by wrapping around and climbing up their thin processes.

The pathway of migration depends both on internal genetic programs and external molecular cues from surrounding cells. Additionally, neuroblasts use **radial glial cells** to guide them to their final destination by wrapping around and climbing up their thin processes (Figure 4.3). In particular, neuroblasts climb along radial glial cells to form layered brain structures, such as the cerebral cortex and the cerebellum. Neuroblasts leaving the neural crest first migrate to a site that will become the deepest layer of the brain. Those neuroblasts that leave the neural crest later on will

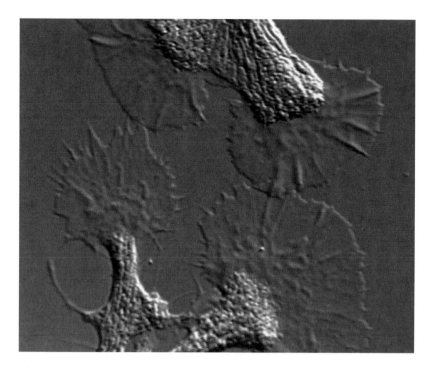

Figure 4.4 This image shows several growth cones of cultured neurons. Note the many finger-like filopodia extending from the growth cones.

migrate to sites closer to the surface of the brain. In this way, the brain is constructed from the inside out.

GROWING AXONS

After the neurons migrate and reach their final destination, the next step is to wire up the appropriate contacts with other neurons and muscles. These contacts are formed by the outgrowth of **neurites**—long, thin membrane projections that will eventually become the dendrites and axon of a neuron—from the cell body. The targets of these growing neurites may be as close as a neighboring neuron or as far away as three feet. At the tip of a growing axon is an elaborate structure called the **growth cone** (Figure 4.4). The growth cone is constantly in motion, extending and retracting small finger-like projections called **filopodia**

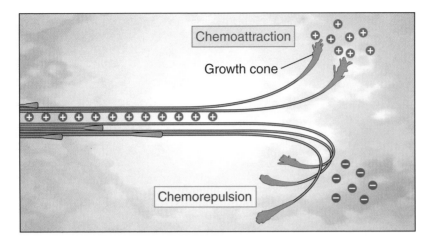

Figure 4.5 Some molecules draw growth cones toward them, which is called chemoattraction. Other molecules push growth cones away from them, which is called chemorepulsion.

as it searches for the correct pathway to the target. These filopodia "sniff around" to help the axon find its way to the target.

A number of factors guide the growth cone in the right direction. These factors include both nondiffusible and diffusible signals in the extracellular environment. The nondiffusible signals are generally special molecules found in the space between cells. These molecules provide adhesive, glue-like forces to stick down the axon as it makes its way to the target. The diffusible signals, which are secreted from nearby cells, also help guide the axon on its way. Diffusible signals include tropic and trophic molecules. **Tropic molecules** are those that physically guide the growth cone (Figure 4.5). Some tropic molecules draw the growth cone toward them in a positive manner by **chemoattraction**. Other tropic molecules push the growth cone away from them in a negative manner by **chemorepulsion**. Just as it is important to tell the axon where to go, it is also important to tell the axon where *not* to go. In contrast to the tropic molecules, **trophic molecules** support the survival and growth of the neurites once the target has been reached. In many cases, trophic molecules are produced by the target muscle or neuron. Among other trophic molecules is a well-studied one called **nerve growth factor** (**NGF**) (see "Discovering Nerve Growth Factor: Rita Levi-Montalcini" box). Like other growth factors, NGF binds to a special receptor on growing neurites and thereby promotes their elaborate growth and survival (Figure 4.6).

Discovering Nerve Growth Factor: Rita Levi-Montalcini

Rita Levi-Montalcini won the Nobel Prize in 1986 for her discovery of the trophic effects of NGF.

Rita Levi-Montalcini is an Italian scientist who is credited with the discovery of the trophic (supportive) qualities of nerve growth factor (NGF) during the 1950s. At the time, Levi-Montalcini was working in the laboratory of Viktor Hamburger at Washington University in St. Louis, Missouri. In her groundbreaking experiments, she found that a substance secreted from a mouse tumor stimulated the survival of certain neurons by causing massive outgrowth of neural processes (see Figure 4.6). Levi-Montalcini then went on to develop an assay to measure the activity of this substance under various conditions. She found that it could exert its growth-stimulating effects in as little as 30 seconds. Later on, Levi-Montalcini and another colleague, Stanley Cohen, isolated and characterized this substance, which turned out to be NGF. In 1986, Levi-Montalcini and Stanley Cohen received the Nobel Prize in Physiology or Medicine, one of the most distinguished scientific awards.

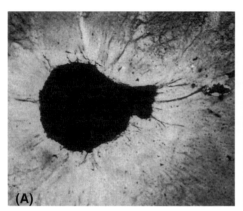
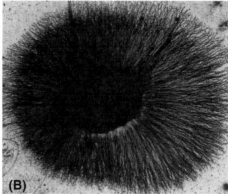

Figure 4.6 **(A)** A ganglion without NGF. **(B)** A ganglion treated with NGF. Note the massive neurite outgrowth that occurs in the presence of NGF.

BUILDING SYNAPSES

Once the growth cone reaches its target, it begins to make the appropriate connections with the target neurons or muscles. Initially, the target is supplied with many more axons than are necessary. Each axon begins forming synapses onto the target. The activity of the new synapses somehow triggers a competition among all the axons that contact a single target. The axons with stronger and more active synaptic connections usually win the competition. All of the weaker axons lose the competition, and in doing so, disconnect their synapses and retract. Thus, it is a "use it or lose it" principle that applies to the pruning of synaptic connections. This process is called **synapse elimination**. Despite the name, this process is actually reducing the number of *axons*, not synapses, onto the target. In contrast to what the name implies, the total number of synapses actually increases during synapse elimination because the winning axon forms many new synaptic connections during the competition (Figure 4.7). In humans, synapse elimination begins only after birth and proceeds over the next 18 months. In the end, synapse elimination ensures that all targets receive input.

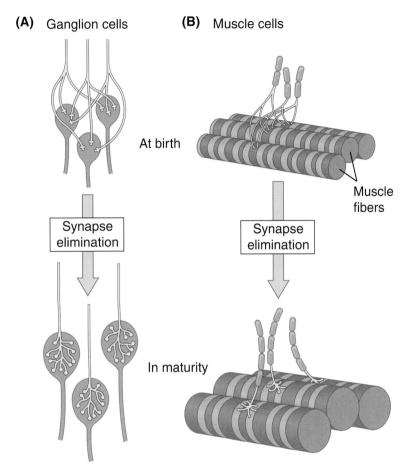

(A) Ganglion cells   **(B)** Muscle cells

At birth

Muscle fibers

Synapse elimination

Synapse elimination

In maturity

Figure 4.7 At birth, neurons and muscles receive multiple axonal inputs. Following synapse elimination, these inputs are reduced to the appropriate number.

After the initial connections are established in the brain, synaptic connections continue to be refined for several years in ways that rely largely on our experiences and our environment. The purpose of these refinements is to help shape our senses and behaviors. For example, both vision and language require certain refinements of synapses before a certain time, or critical period, has passed. Furthermore, the synapses involved in learning and memory continue to be refined throughout life. Clearly, even after the brain is formed, there is still much work to be done.

5 Synaptic Plasticity: The Changing Brain

For many years, researchers believed that the nervous system did not change after its initial wiring during development. This notion turned out to be far from true. Although there are no large-scale changes in the nervous system following development, many smaller modifications continue throughout one's lifetime. Most of these modifications occur at the level of the synapse and are dependent on its level of activity, or how much it is used. Modifications of synapse structure and function are collectively called **synaptic plasticity**. Synaptic plasticity can be short-lived or long-term. It can result in a change in synapse strength or synapse number. In some special cases, new neurons can be added to the brain's circuitry. Because the effects of synaptic plasticity can last for a long time, this process is thought to underlie learning and memory. In this chapter, you will learn about the different types of synaptic plasticity and their mechanisms. Keep in mind that the active brain is always changing (see "The Teen Brain: A Work in Progress" box).

■ **Learn more about the adolescent brain** Search the Internet for *teen brain*.

CHANGES IN SYNAPSE STRENGTH

One way that the mature brain changes is by altering the strength of preexisting synapses. Such changes in synapse strength can be either short-term or long-term and can either increase or decrease the response of the synapse.

Short-term plasticity comes in several forms (Figure 5.1). One type of short-term change that increases the response of a synapse is called **facilitation**. Facilitation occurs when more than one action potential reaches the nerve terminal within a short period of time, resulting in more and more neurotransmitter release with each action potential. Eventually, the system becomes overwhelmed and the nerve terminal cannot efficiently recycle

The Teen Brain: A Work in Progress

At times, your parents may question your choices or your judgment. They may complain that something extraordinary is going on in your brain. Well, it's true. And now, you can tell them exactly what it is. During early development, the brain undergoes a period of growth followed by a period of pruning connections. For a long time, it was assumed that once the brain had developed, it was finished. However, recent evidence shows that the brain undergoes a second wave of synapse sprouting during puberty. This is followed by a period of pruning synapses during the teen years, which presumably occurs to get rid of unused connections. These changes are especially rich within regions of the brain that are involved in planning, judgment, creativity, and emotions. Therefore, it is likely that the growth spurt in the teen brain helps make the proper connections between neurons in these regions. Scientists believe that the "use it or lose it" principle also applies to the new connections in the teen brain. That is, if you spend time reading, playing sports, or making music, these connections will get hardwired. So, use your time wisely.

SHORT-TERM SYNAPTIC PLASTICITY

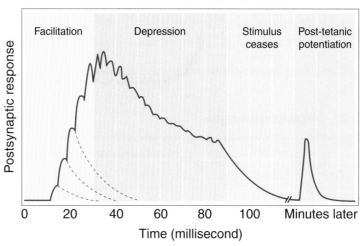

Figure 5.1 This graph shows different kinds of short-term plasticity.

synaptic vesicles, resulting in a decrease of neurotransmitter release. This is called **synaptic depression**. Both facilitation and
synaptic depression are short-lived and usually last less than one
second. Following a high-frequency burst of action potentials (a
"tetanus") such as that which causes facilitation and synaptic depression, the nerve terminal may retain the capacity to release
more neurotransmitter for several minutes. This is called **post-
tetanic potentiation**. All these types of short-term plasticity are
caused by changes in the presynaptic nerve terminal. Because
short-term plasticity is transient, it is unlikely to mediate long-
lasting changes in the brain's circuitry, such as those that occur
during the storage of memories, which can last for many years.

Long-term synaptic plasticity also comes in several forms.
However, the mechanisms that underlie long-term synaptic
plasticity are quite different from those that underlie short-term
plasticity. For example, long-term synaptic plasticity involves
changes on the postsynaptic side of the synapse—that is, the

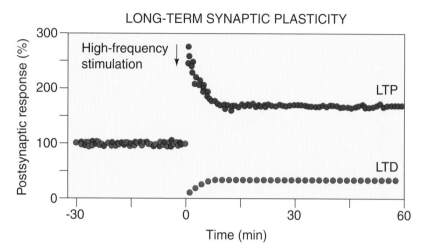

Figure 5.2 A long-lasting increase in synaptic response that can last up to or more than an hour is called long-term potentiation (purple). A long-lasting decrease in the response is called long-term depression (green).

dendrite. Sometimes, repeated, high-frequency synaptic activity causes an increase in the synaptic response that can last up to or more than an hour. This is called **long-term potentiation**, or **LTP**. In contrast, when repeated synaptic activity causes a long-lasting decrease in the response, it is called **long-term depression**, or **LTD**. During LTP and LTD, only the active synapses undergo a change in strength, whereas the inactive synapses remain unchanged. In other words, there is **synapse specificity.** Furthermore, an active synapse will only become strengthened or weakened if another neighboring pathway is activated at the same time. In these cases, the strength of both pathways changes. This feature is called **associativity.** Compared to short-term plasticity, which lasts for less than a minute, LTP and LTD last for hours or days (Figure 5.2). In these ways, LTP and LTD are reminiscent of learning and memory and may therefore be the mechanisms that underlie such important brain functions.

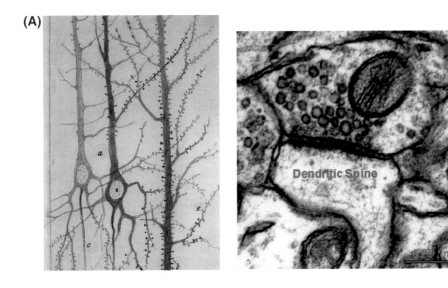

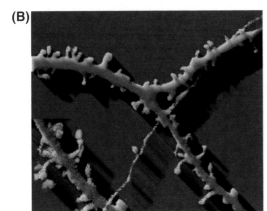

Figure 5.3 (A) Drawing by Ramón y Cajal showing many spines (black projections) on a dendrite. **(B)** Three-dimensional reconstruction of a dendrite with spines. Note their many shapes and sizes. **(C)** Electron micrograph showing a spine contacting a nerve terminal.

Changes in synapse strength associated with LTP and LTD occur within a special part of the dendrite called the **spine** (Figure 5.3). Many spines have a wide, bulbous head attached to the shaft of the dendrite by a thin neck. The shape of the spine may be important for concentrating special molecules that are needed during synaptic plasticity. Recent studies of dendritic spines have revealed one mechanism that explains how LTP and

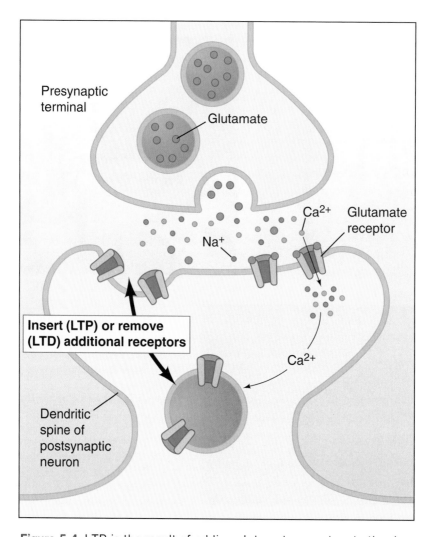

Figure 5.4 LTP is the result of adding glutamate receptors to the dendritic spine, making the synapse more responsive to glutamate. LTD is the result of removing receptors, making the synapse less responsive to glutamate.

LTD occur. Repeated activity of the kind that causes LTP triggers a cascade of events within the spine that ultimately leads to the addition of more glutamate receptors (Figure 5.4). As a result, the synapse is more sensitive to the next packet of glutamate released from the presynaptic nerve terminal. Similarly, repeated activity of the kind that causes LTD removes glutamate receptors, thereby decreasing the sensitivity of the synapse.

Although LTP and LTD do not explain everything that we know about learning and memory, they currently offer the best explanation for what occurs in the synapse during these processes. To add further support, LTP and LTD occur in many brain regions involved in learning and memory, including the hippocampus, the cortex, the amygdala, and the cerebellum.

CHANGES IN SYNAPSE NUMBER

Over the past decade, researchers have uncovered another exciting way that synaptic connections can be modified in the mature brain. In addition to changes in synapse strength, there are also modifications of brain circuits that alter the total number of synapses. This was a great surprise, indeed. Much like changes in synapse strength, structural modifications depend on the prior experience and activity of the synapse.

Together, researchers Jon Kaas (of Vanderbilt University in Nashville, Tennessee) and Michael Merzenich (of the University of California in San Francisco, California) made one of the first observations hinting that structural modifications occur in the adult mammalian brain. In their experiment, they cut the nerve to the middle finger of an owl monkey—a sort of amputation—thereby making it immobile. Two months later, they took recordings from the brain of the monkey. Normally, the brain devotes equal space to each finger (see Chapter 6). However, in the monkey with the amputated finger, the brain areas responding to the second and fourth finger had taken over the area that normally responded to the immobile middle finger. Therefore, the mature brain had modified its synapses according to experience. Because these modifications covered such a large area of the brain, the best explanation was a physical rearrangement of the synapses or an addition of new synapses. Sim-

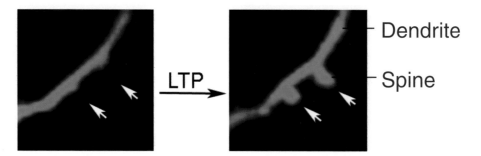

Figure 5.5 Synapse number in the adult brain can be modified. For example, LTP can induce the formation of new dendritic spines.

ilar to what happens during nervous system development, the synaptic rearrangement in the mature brain follows the "use it or lose it" principle. Very recent studies have revealed that new synapses can be generated in the mature nervous system. For example, additional dendritic spines can be generated after the induction of LTP (Figure 5.5). Similarly, LTD causes spine shrinkage or loss. These postsynaptic changes are likely paralleled by addition and removal of presynaptic nerve terminals. In these ways, our brains are constantly changing in order to incorporate our experiences.

CHANGES IN NEURON NUMBER

Mature neurons do not divide. Therefore, for many years, researchers believed that the mature brain was incapable of making new neurons. What a surprise it was to discover that the adult brain could indeed generate new neurons from neural stem cells. These neural stem cells originate from a region of the brain called the **subventricular zone**. Similar to what happens during development (see Chapter 4), the neural stem cells in the adult brain can divide, and each daughter cell can become either a neuron or a glial cell. However, there are many fewer neural stem cells produced in the adult brain. Furthermore, the use of neural stem cells to make new neurons seems to be limited to a few brain regions. There remains much to learn about neurogenesis in the adult brain.

As you can see, our brains continue to change even after development. Synapses are strengthened and weakened, made and removed. Our experiences continue to shape these intricate synaptic connections for the rest of our lives. So, with regard to your brain, be sure to "use it" before you "lose it."

6 The Senses: Making "Sense" of It All

Your ability to sense things in the environment is due to the performance of your nervous system. The nervous system receives light waves that enter your eyes and translates them into images that you see. Similarly, the nervous system translates sound waves, airborne molecules, ingested molecules, and mechanical forces into what you hear, smell, taste, and touch. Separate neural pathways, or systems, process each type of sensory information. Although the inputs are different, there are similarities in how the sensory systems process them. For example, each sensory system has specialized receptors located in the periphery that detect the stimulus, whether it consists of light, sound, airborne molecules, ingested molecules, or mechanical forces. Furthermore, each sensory system has the ability to translate the stimulus into an electrical signal that the nervous system can understand. Several sensory systems can even interpret the strength and location of the input—for example, whether a sound is loud or soft and whether it is coming from the right or the left. In this chapter, you will learn about the sensory systems and how they help us see, hear, smell, taste, and touch.

SEEING: THE VISUAL SYSTEM

The visual system is responsible for interpreting the size, shape, color, location, orientation, and movement of everything that

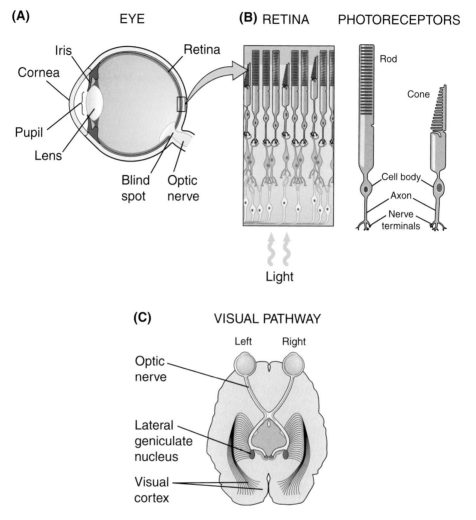

(A) EYE

Iris
Cornea
Pupil
Lens
Retina
Blind spot
Optic nerve

(B) RETINA PHOTORECEPTORS

Rod
Cone
Cell body
Axon
Nerve terminals

Light

(C) VISUAL PATHWAY

Left   Right

Optic nerve
Lateral geniculate nucleus
Visual cortex

Figure 6.1 The visual system consists of the eyes, the retina, the optic nerve, and the visual pathways of the nervous system that allow light to be decoded and translated into an image.

you see. It consists of the eyes, the retina, the optic nerve, and the brain regions that allow an image to be decoded and perceived. Vision begins with the eye (Figure 6.1A). Light reflected from an object enters the eye through a clear tissue on the front surface called the **cornea**. It then passes through a hole called the **pupil**, the size of which is controlled by a colored muscle called the **iris**. Next, the **lens** focuses the light—and thus, the image—onto the **retina** at the back of the eye.

Although situated in the periphery, the retina is considered a part of the central nervous system because it consists of several layers of neurons (Figure 6.1B). One layer of the retina contains **photoreceptors**, which, as their name implies, are neurons that detect photons (particles) of light. The two types of photoreceptors are called **cones** and **rods**. Cones are sensitive to bright light and color. They are active during normal vision. Rods are sensitive to dim light and insensitive to color. Thus, they are most active during night vision. The human retina contains 90 million rods and 5 million cones. Animals that can see in color, such as monkeys, cats, many fish, and insects, have both cones and rods in their retinas. Many nocturnal animals, such as hawks and mice, do not see in color because their retinas contain only rods. Like other neurons, photoreceptors have cell bodies, axons, and nerve terminals. In place of dendrites, photoreceptors have a single, thick structure that houses membrane stacks that are filled with light-sensitive molecules called **photopigments**. Light activates photopigments, thereby triggering a molecular cascade inside the photoreceptors. This cascade ultimately changes the amount of neurotransmitter released from the photoreceptor nerve terminals, thereby altering the activity of neighboring neurons within the other retinal layers (Figure 6.1B). (These other retinal neurons decode information about color and contrast of objects.) Several known medical conditions are associated with abnormal photoreceptor function. For example, **color blindness** is the result of a genetic defect in photopigment production, which causes an inability to distinguish red from green. This condition affects 5% to 6% of American males. **Macular degeneration** is a common aging-related condition in which photoreceptors die, resulting in dramatic loss of vision.

Besides interpreting the shape, color, and contrast of an object, the retina interprets the position of the object in space. The retina is capable of doing this because it maintains an orderly representation of visual space across its surface. For example, when looking at your hand, the visual information about your thumb is always processed on the retina next to the information about your pointer finger. This type of organization is referred to as a **retinotopic**, or **visual**, **map**. This visual map is retained at each step of processing in the visual system from the retina all the way to the brain (refer back to Figure 6.1C). That way, orderly images do not have to be reassembled from jumbled parts. Visual information leaves the retina via the **optic nerve**, a collection of axons arising from neurons in the retina (see "Visual Trickery: How You Can 'See' Your Blind Spot" box). Many axons of the optic nerve project to the opposite side from which they originate while others remain on the same side, ensuring that each half of the brain receives input from both eyes. The first stop in the brain is a region deep within the forebrain called the **lateral geniculate nucleus**, where the nerve terminals coming from the left and right eye are separated into distinct layers. Visual information is then passed along to a region of the occipital lobe called the **visual cortex**, which interprets information about the orientation and color of objects. The visual cortex then passes the information to other associated brain regions that decode more details about the shape, size, texture, and direction of movement of the object. Finally, the brain puts all the features back together to give you an exact impression of what you see.

HEARING: THE AUDITORY SYSTEM

The auditory system is responsible for interpreting the source, location, and meaning of everything that you hear—including speech, music, cars, sirens, and machines. It consists of the ears, cochlea, auditory nerve, and brain regions that decode sounds and translate them into what you hear. Sounds are compressed air waves. The pitch of the sound is determined by the frequency of the sound waves. That is, high-pitched sounds, such as those made by sirens, are made by high-frequency sound waves. Low-pitched sounds, such as those made by bulldozers, are made by

Visual Trickery: How You Can "See" Your Blind Spot

X   ●

———————————————————

━━━ ━━━ ━━━   X

Follow the instructions in this box to reveal the blind spot.

Everyone has a blind spot on his or her retina at the place where the optic nerve leaves the eye. Light that is focused onto the blind spot is not seen because there are no photoreceptors there. You do not notice your blind spot when observing an object. Instead, the blind spot is filled in with information from surrounding areas. You can reveal your blind spot and the filling-in phenomenon using two simple visual tricks. First, close your left eye and stare at the cross mark with your right eye (top diagram). Hold this book about 40 cm (15.7 inches) away from you. Then, *slowly* move the book toward you and you will see the spot disappear. The point where you can no longer see the spot is when it is in the visual path of your blind spot. Move the book closer toward you and the spot will reappear. Now try another trick (bottom diagram). This time, close your right eye and stare at the cross mark with your left eye. Again, hold the book about 40 cm (15.7 inches) from you and start moving it slowly toward you until you see the break in the line disappear. This trick illustrates how information from surrounding regions fills in the blind spot.

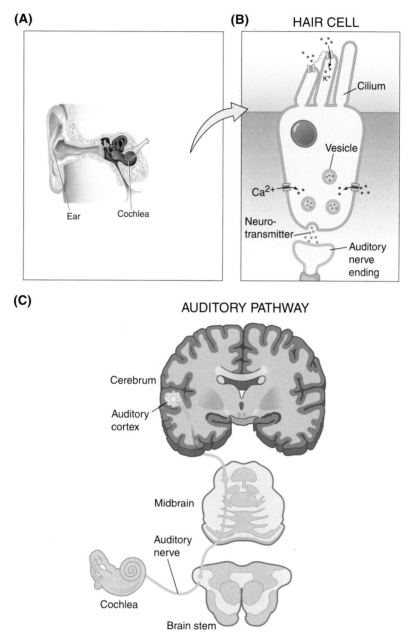

Figure 6.2 The auditory system consists of **(A)** the ears and the cochlea, **(B)** auditory nerve, and **(C)** auditory pathways that decode sounds and translate them into what you hear.

low-frequency sound waves. Hearing begins with the ear (Figure 6.2A). The outer ear captures and concentrates the sound waves. Then, the sound waves are transmitted across the **tympanic membrane** (also called the eardrum) to three small bones of the middle ear, which are called **ossicles**. The ossicles transmit the sound waves as vibrations to a part of the inner ear called the **cochlea**. The cochlea's job is to convert the vibrations into signals that the brain can understand.

Within the cochlea is an array of neurons that are sensitive to sound vibrations. These neurons are referred to as **hair cells** because they have special thin, hair-like extensions called **cilia** on their upper surface (Figure 6.2B). The cilia move back and forth at the same frequency as the sound vibrations. Each hair cell is tuned to respond to a specific frequency of sound vibration, similar to a tuning fork. The cilia movements generate action potentials in the hair cells, triggering neurotransmitter release onto auditory nerve endings. Neurotransmitter release from human hair cells can match cilia movements up to 3,000 Hz frequencies. Because of this, the auditory system is the fastest sensory system of all. Deafness is often caused by a loss in the number or the function of hair cells, which can occur as the result of disease or prolonged environmental stress, such as working with loud equipment or listening to loud music. Earplugs can protect your hair cells from such damage.

The cochlea maintains an orderly representation of sound frequencies across its surface by arranging the hair cells according to the sound frequencies to which they are tuned. For example, hair cells that respond to high frequencies are located at the beginning of the cochlea, while those that respond to low frequencies are located at the end of the cochlea. This type of organization is referred to as a **tonotopic (tone) map**. Like the retinotopic map in the visual system, the tonotopic map is retained at each step of processing in the auditory system from the cochlea all the way to the brain.

Auditory information leaves the cochlea via the **auditory nerve**, a collection of axons coming from the cochlea (Figure 6.2C). Axons of the auditory nerve project to both sides of the brain, ensuring that each side of the brain receives input from the two ears. The first stop in the brain is the brain stem. Here, the location and the duration of the sound are computed. The brain stem then sends the information through the midbrain to the **auditory cortex**, where complex sequences of sounds, such as speech and music, are processed. Other associated brain regions process additional features of the sound. Finally, the brain puts all the features together to give you an exact impression of what you hear.

TOUCHING: THE SOMATOSENSORY SYSTEM

The somatosensory system (*soma* means "body") is responsible for interpreting the location, texture, and quality of everything that comes into contact with the surface of your body. The somatosensory system detects light mechanical touch on the body's surface, such as a tap on the shoulder or the feeling of your clothes. It also detects painful touch, such as a pinprick, a burn, or a cut. The somatosensory system includes the somatosensory receptors on the skin, peripheral sensory nerves, and brain regions that interpret the touch information and then trigger the appropriate reaction (Figure 6.3). The sensation of touch begins when something contacts the skin. The skin contains special **somatosensory receptors**, which can be classified into several categories (Figure 6.3A). Some receptors detect sensations about changes in the skin's shape—for example, during light touch, vibration, pressure, and stretch on the skin. Other receptors detect sensations of pain. Still other receptors detect sensations of temperature. Because somatosensory receptors are specialized for detecting different types of touch, the information leaving the skin is already highly processed.

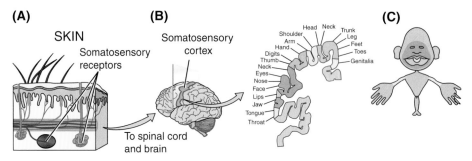

Figure 6.3 The somatosensory system includes **(A)** the somatosensory receptors on the skin, neurons that carry information through the spinal cord, and **(B)** the somatosensory cortex of the brain. **(C)** This drawing illustrates the relative size of body parts as they are represented in the brain.

Somatosensory receptors are physically associated with nerve endings of sensory neurons. When something touches the skin, the somatosensory receptors trigger action potentials in the nerve endings that are carried to the spinal cord. The spinal cord then transmits the information to the brain stem, which, in turn, transmits the information to a region of the forebrain called the **somatosensory cortex** (Figure 6.3B). The neurons of the somatosensory cortex are maintained as an orderly representation of the body's surface, or a **somatotopic map**. Within the cortex, however, the body's surface is not equally represented. For example, the region of the somatosensory cortex that processes information coming from the face and the hands is much larger than that which processes information coming from other body parts. This is because the face and hands have a greater density of somatosensory receptors than other parts of the body (Figure 6.3C). Other associated brain regions process additional features of the touch. Finally, the brain puts all the features together to give you a perception of a sensation on your skin and then prepares the body's reaction. Although a large part of touch and pain sensation is generated in the peripheral nervous system, the central nervous system participates greatly in the perception. An illustration of this is the **phantom limb**, or phantom pain, phenomenon experienced by amputees. Amputees often perceive a phantom limb where the hand, arm, or leg used to be. Sometimes, there is a sensation of tingling, burning, or pain in the area of the missing limb. Because there is no input from the periphery, these sensations are generated entirely by the central nervous system.

SMELLING: THE OLFACTORY SYSTEM

The olfactory system is responsible for interpreting the identity and intensity of everything that you smell. It consists of the nose, olfactory epithelium, and brain regions that detect airborne molecules and translate them into what you smell (Figure 6.4). Airborne molecules that are detected by the nose and that often produce a smell are called **odorants**. Odorants originate from food, one's body, other people, and objects in our surroundings. Therefore, the sense of smell can influence many important nutritional, social, and reproductive behaviors. Smelling begins with the nose when airborne molecules enter and are detected by special receptor neurons on the olfactory epithelium (Figure 6.4A). The **olfactory epithelium** is a sheet of cells within the nasal cavity made of neurons and supporting cells. The neurons, called **olfactory receptor neurons**, contain special **odorant receptor** molecules on their surface. Humans have between 1,000 and 2,000 different kinds of odorant receptors, providing one possible explanation for the fact that humans can distinguish up to 10,000 different smells. Binding of an odorant to its specific receptor triggers a molecular cascade, which leads to neurotransmitter release from the nerve terminals of olfactory receptor neurons. The amount of neurotransmitter released is proportional to the concentration of the odorant—the stronger the odorant, the more neurotransmitter

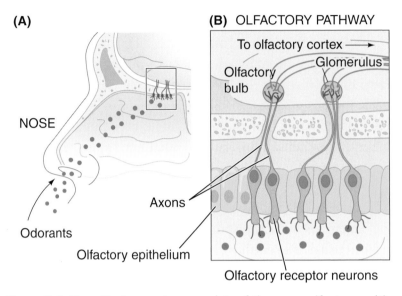

(A)

(B) OLFACTORY PATHWAY

To olfactory cortex

Glomerulus

Olfactory bulb

NOSE

Axons

Odorants

Olfactory epithelium

Olfactory receptor neurons

Figure 6.4 The olfactory system consists of the nose, olfactory epithelium, and olfactory pathways that detect airborne molecules and translate them into what you smell.

is released. Unlike most other neurons, olfactory receptor neurons continually die and are replaced. Surprisingly, the entire population of olfactory receptor neurons turns over every 6 to 8 weeks in some mammals.

Information leaves the olfactory epithelium via the axons arising from the olfactory receptor neurons (Figure 6.4B). These axons project to a region of the forebrain called the **olfactory bulb**. Neurons that express the same kind of receptor converge upon and form synapses with a small cluster of neurons called a **glomerulus** (plural is *glomeruli*). Neurons of the olfactory bulb project from the olfactory bulb to other parts of the forebrain, which include the **olfactory cortex**, the amygdala, and the hypothalamus. These areas probably process other features of the odorant, such as emotions and memories attached to a particular smell. Associated brain regions process other features of the odorant. Finally, the brain puts all the

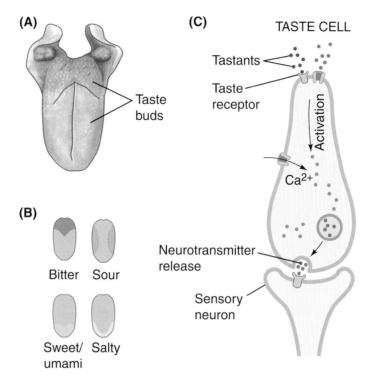

(A)

Taste buds

(B)

Bitter   Sour

Sweet/ Salty
umami

(C)   TASTE CELL

Tastants

Taste receptor

Activation

Ca^{2+}

Neurotransmitter release

Sensory neuron

Figure 6.5 The taste system consists of the tongue, taste buds, taste cells, and neural pathways to the brain that process and identify taste information.

features together to give you an exact impression of what you smell.

TASTING: THE TASTE SYSTEM

The taste system is responsible for interpreting the identity and intensity of ingested molecules, most of which are in the foods we eat. It helps us distinguish the sweetness of fruit and the unpleasant qualities of spoiled food. Thus, taste is important not only for the enjoyment of food but also for our health. The taste system consists of the tongue, taste buds, and brain regions that process taste information (Figure 6.5). Taste begins when food is chewed and mixed with saliva, a process that begins breaking down food into its individual molecular components. Ingested molecules, called **tastants**, are detected by special neurons located within the taste buds called **taste cells**. Taste cells contain **taste receptors** on their surface. The different kinds of taste receptors are classified according to whether they give rise to a bitter, sour, sweet, savory or salty taste (Figure 6.5B). Savory taste is also called *umami*, the Japanese word for "delicious." When tastants

Animals With Amazing Senses

As humans, we rely heavily on our sense of vision for survival. Visual cues help us find food, choose mates, and interpret the behavior of others. In contrast, many animals use other senses as their main mode for survival. For example, bats and dolphins use a special type of hearing called echolocation to detect their prey. To do so, they produce high-frequency sound waves. Then, the sound waves reflect off an object and are detected by the ears or other sense organs. These reflected sound waves convey information about the location and size of the prey. Whereas humans can hear sound waves with frequencies between 20 and 20,000 Hz, bats can hear sounds between 3,000 and 120,000 Hz—an amazing range. In contrast, bees cannot hear or see very well. Instead, they use their sense of smell to locate food, mates, and home. Mosquitoes also use their sense of smell to find a host. Popular mosquito repellants often contain a compound called **DEET**, which disrupts the mosquito's sense of smell and, hence, its ability to find you. Butterflies, on the other hand, find food by using taste receptors located on their feet. A cockroach can detect movements up to 2,000 times smaller than a hydrogen atom, using their sense of touch. As you can see, many animals have amazing senses that help them in a variety of survival tasks.

bind to the receptors, they trigger a molecular cascade inside the taste cell that leads to the release of neurotransmitter onto sensory neurons. Tastants perceived as sweet, bitter, and umami trigger a different molecular cascade from those perceived as sour and salty.

Activated sensory neurons then carry the taste information to the brain stem. The brain stem then sends the information to the gustatory (taste) cortex and other regions of the brain. The brain processes information regarding the identity and intensity of the taste as well as information about being hungry or full. In doing so, it gives you an exact impression of what you taste.

As you can see, the nervous system is exclusively designed for translating and transmitting sensory information from the environment. In addition to the brain regions that process each individual sense, there are many other parts of the brain that integrate information coming in through several sensory systems. For example, some regions simultaneously process both visual and auditory input. All of these neural sensory systems work together to help you move through the world, find food, and communicate with others (see "Animals With Amazing Senses" box). Thus, the proper functioning of our sensory systems is crucial for daily human survival.

■ **Learn more about the senses** Search the Internet for the *five senses* and *nervous systems*.

7 Injury and Repair

It is not uncommon to sustain an unplanned hit in the head during a sports game or while roughhousing with a sibling. Perhaps you know someone who had whiplash as a result of a car accident. In many cases, thankfully, the impact from these incidents produces no damage to the central nervous system because of the heavy protection afforded by the bones of the skull and the vertebrae. However, sometimes a hit is hard enough to injure the nervous system and cause permanent brain damage or paralysis. Likewise, perhaps you know someone who has had a stroke. If so, you probably realize that a stroke can also cause long-lasting damage to the brain; the person may become unable to speak or move properly. Thus, the nervous system has the potential for serious injury.

The results of injury to the nervous system can be permanent and devastating. Although the impact of the initial primary injury on the nervous system is great, the damage does not end there. Most injuries also set off a secondary response within the damaged neurons and glial cells. Though secondary responses are intended to help repair the nervous system, they can also cause further damage to neurons and glia. In this chapter, you will learn about some common types of nervous system injuries and how the neurons and glia respond to them. You will also learn how the nervous system can occasionally repair itself.

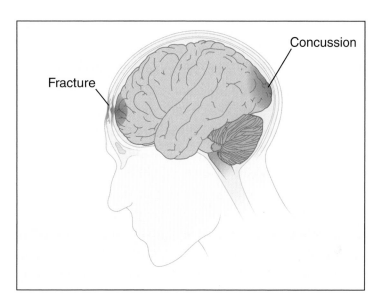

Figure 7.1 A concussion is a closed head injury where the damage is kept confined within the skull. In contrast, a fracture is a penetrating head injury where an object breaks open the skull and enters the brain.

TYPES OF NERVOUS SYSTEM INJURIES
Traumatic Brain Injury

Each year, 1 million Americans sustain a traumatic brain injury (Figure 7.1). Of those, 230,000 have to be hospitalized and 99,000 have some kind of permanent brain damage. Men are twice as likely as women to sustain a traumatic brain injury, with the highest risk occurring between the ages of 15 and 24. Because such brain injuries can result in permanent damage, young people affected by brain damage may need sustained care for the rest of their lives. Thus, the total cost for health care following a traumatic brain injury can be astronomical. More important, the injury dramatically impacts the quality of life for the individual and takes a huge toll on his or her loved ones and caregivers.

There are several classes of traumatic brain injuries. A **closed head injury** occurs when the damage is kept confined within the skull, such as that which occurs as a result of a **concussion**. Many closed head injuries result in minor and reversible brain damage. In contrast, a penetrating head injury, or **fracture**, occurs when an object breaks open the skull and enters the brain. Penetrating head injuries can cause major permanent brain damage, including coma and even death. However, either type of brain injury has the potential to cause widespread damage if it causes heavy bleeding within the brain. The most common causes of traumatic brain injury are vehicle accidents and sports-related activities. Initial signs of traumatic brain injury include headache, blurred vision, nausea, confusion, and memory impairment. Over the long term, people who have suffered traumatic brain injury may lose some ability for high-level thought processes, movements, and sensation. In the most severe cases, the person may become depressed or experience a change in personality. Traumatic brain injuries often require immediate treatment to control the bleeding in the brain and to relieve the increased pressure on the skull that occurs as a result of brain swelling. In these cases, surgery offers the best option for stabilizing the brain. Many traumatic brain injuries can be avoided with proper safety precautions. Next time you decide to go for a ride on your bicycle, be sure to wear your helmet.

Spinal Cord Injury

Spinal cord injuries represent another kind of traumatic distress to the nervous system. When the vertebrae of the spine sustain a sudden, blunt force, there is a high risk of injuring the neuronal axons encased within them (Figure 7.2). The most common causes of spinal cord injuries are vehicle-related and sports-related accidents and violence (see "The Life of a Truly Super Man: Christopher Reeve" box). More than 10,000 Americans experience spinal cord injuries each year. An estimated 200,000 Amer-

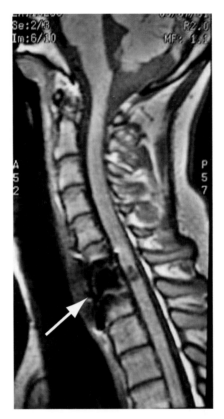

Figure 7.2 An MRI shows the position of a spinal cord injury (*arrow*).

icans are living with disability as a result of vehicle- and sports-related injuries. As with traumatic brain injuries, the vast majority of spinal cord injuries occur in people in their early 20s. Therefore, lifetime costs of treating the injury and caring for the individual can be very high, often exceeding $250,000 per year.

There are several types of primary spinal cord injuries. These include those that compress or bruise the spinal cord. Sometimes, the spinal cord is severed, or broken. Although the impact of spinal cord injury is immediate, the majority of the damage is often caused by other secondary effects. These secondary effects include demyelination of the axons in the spinal cord, axon

The Life of a Truly Super Man: Christopher Reeve

Christopher Reeve
(1952–2004)

Christopher Reeve, actor and human rights advocate, was born on September 25, 1952. After attending Juilliard, Reeve expanded his stage career to include television, Broadway plays, and movies. His breakout role came in 1978 when he was cast as the lead role in the movie *Superman®*. He also starred in 17 feature films, a dozen television movies, and about 150 plays. In addition to acting, Reeve was a political activist supporting issues such as the environment, funding for the arts, and First Amendment rights. In May 1995, Reeve was thrown from his horse while riding in a competition. The fall injured his spinal cord at the uppermost vertebrae and completely paralyzed him from the neck down. Following the injury, he was able to return home, but he needed constant care and assistance. This raised his awareness of the needs of people with spinal cord injuries and other disabilities. As a result, in 1996, he founded the Christopher Reeve Paralysis Foundation, an organization that sponsors scientific research on the spinal cord and its regeneration. He also helped raise public awareness about spinal cord injuries and advocated an increase in government funding for such research. Eventually, Reeve regained some sensation down his spine, leg, and arm, and some movement in one index finger, wrist, and thumb. Christopher Reeve died on October 10, 2004, after he went into a coma while being treated for an infection. But his foundation continues to avidly support spinal cord research.

degradation, and neuronal death (discussed later in this chapter). Because the spinal cord carries signals from the brain to the rest of the body, the consequences of a spinal cord injury can be very dramatic. If the injury destroys the axons of motor neurons, there is a high risk for losing movement in the arms or legs. If the injury destroys sensory neurons, there is a high risk for losing the ability to sense touch, pressure, and temperature. Because different segments of the spinal cord feed information to different regions of the body, the position of the spinal cord injury can also determine the severity of the damage. For example, if a person sustains damage near the top of the spinal cord at the base of the brain, he or she might die because these axons regulate processes that are crucial for sustaining life, such as breathing and digestion. On the other hand, a person who sustains damage to the lowest region of the spinal cord may experience paralysis of the legs, but retain full use of the arms and hands.

Over the past 20 years, scientists and doctors have learned a great deal about how to treat spinal cord injuries. Currently, the treatment for a spinal cord injury takes a three-fold approach. First, any pressure on the spinal cord must be relieved. Next, the secondary effects such as inflammation must be reduced. To be successful, these treatments must usually be applied within eight hours of the initial injury. Finally, steps must be taken to prevent another similar injury. Once the person is stabilized, he or she will go through physical therapy training to help regain some of the ability to move and to maintain the flexibility and strength that remains. Recent advances in technology have allowed the development of electrodes that can be implanted into patients to stimulate muscle contractions. Using these devices, patients can sometimes overcome the paralysis and relearn how to regain some control of their muscles.

■ **Learn more about spinal cord injury** Search the Internet for *Christopher Reeve* and *spinal cord injury.*

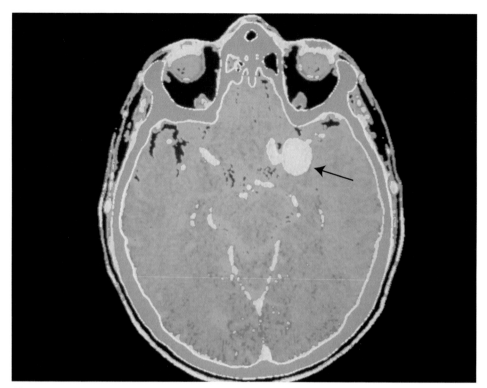

Figure 7.3 The arrow shows the position of a stroke in the right frontal lobe.

Stroke: An Attack on the Brain

The brain uses between 15% and 20% of the body's oxygen supply. If this oxygen supply to the brain is somehow cut off, the effects can be devastating. A **stroke** occurs when a blood clot blocks an artery and prevents oxygen from reaching the brain. Each year, more than 600,000 Americans have strokes. Furthermore, there are an estimated 160,000 annual deaths from strokes, making it the third largest killer in our country.

Most strokes are caused by a blockage of an artery in the neck or the brain, which prevents the oxygenated blood from reaching the brain (Figure 7.3). This type of stroke is called an ischemic stroke. Alternatively, strokes can be caused by the sudden rupture of an artery, causing massive bleeding in the brain. This type of stroke is called a hemmorhagic stroke. In a split second, a stroke can cause any or all of the following symptoms: numbness or weakness, blurry vision, slurred speech, a splitting headache, confusion, or dizziness. In most cases, the stroke physically affects only one side of the body. For example, someone may suddenly lose his or her ability to move the right arm while the left arm remains unaffected. Or, the left side of the mouth—but not the right—will droop as a result of the stroke. Strokes are typically treated immediately by giving the person medications to dissolve the blood clot that is preventing the oxygenated blood from reaching the brain. In addition, the person may be put on medications to thin the blood to prevent another stroke.

The effects of a stroke may last for weeks, months, or even years. The long-term effects depend largely on the size of the brain area that is affected and the extent of the initial brain damage. In some cases, the effects are both drastic and long-lasting. For example, stroke victims may need long-term physical therapy to help them regain their ability to walk or move their limbs. They may need occupational therapy to help them relearn how to perform everyday activities, such as eating and dressing. Stroke victims may also need speech therapy to help them relearn how to speak and read. Risk factors for stroke include high blood pressure, heart disease, cigarette smoking, diabetes, previous history, or a family history of strokes. Use of oral contraceptives is also a risk factor for stroke in women. In many cases, these risk factors can be controlled with medication or by making intelligent life choices. We all have the ability to reduce our chances of having a stroke in the future by not smoking and by eating healthy foods.

Mini-stroke

A **transient ischemic attack**, or **TIA**, is also known as a mini-stroke. Similar to a stroke, the main cause of TIA is a blocked artery that prevents oxygen flow to the brain. However, TIAs are typically shorter, usually lasting for less than five minutes. The average TIA is complete within one minute. The outward signs of a TIA are virtually indistinguishable from those of a stroke. Therefore, someone who has a TIA should receive treatment immediately. However, unlike a stroke, the effects of a TIA usually disappear within one hour to one day. The risk factors for having a TIA are the same as those for stroke. Recurring TIAs often indicate that a person is at risk for a full-blown stroke. Therefore, all measures should be taken to reduce controllable risk factors.

SECONDARY RESPONSES TO NERVOUS SYSTEM INJURY
The Immune Response

Injury to the nervous system triggers a response from the body's immune system. The immune system's job is to fight infection and reduce inflammation at the site of injury. Normally, the cells of the immune system are kept out of the nervous system because they cannot cross over the blood-brain barrier (see Chapter 3). However, an injury to the nervous system usually causes some disturbance or break in the blood-brain barrier, allowing the immune system cells to enter freely. Most of what is known about the immune response in the nervous system comes from studies of spinal cord injury. Here, the first responders of the immune system are called **neutrophils**. Neutrophils arrive within the first 12 hours after the initial injury. After about 3 days, **T cells** enter the injured site. Normally, T cells help to kill disease-causing organisms that invade the body. However, their exact role in the response to spinal cord injury is unknown. Later, other immune cells called macrophages and monocytes enter the wound. At some point, they are joined by the immune cells of the nervous system—that is, the microglia. Microglia gobble up dead cell debris and secrete substances called cytokines in response to the injury (see Chapter 3). Although some cytokines promote repair of the injured site, others can cause further damage. Which cytokines are secreted, how many of them, and whether they will have positive or negative effects on repairing the spinal cord are still somewhat unclear. In addition to the overproduction of cytokines, activation of the immune response can also generate other harmful by-products, such as free radicals, that can further damage the nervous system.

Excitotoxicity: Neurons in Overdrive

Another consequence of nervous system injury is the massive release of neurotransmitters, which occurs when neurons are damaged. Massive release of the excitatory neurotransmitter glutamate produces a harmful effect on neurons known as **excitotoxicity**. This massive dumping of glutamate overstimulates those neurons that contain glutamate receptors and allows too much calcium to enter the cell (see Chapter 2). Calcium regulates many cellular processes, and these all get turned on at once during excitotoxicity. One consequence of this is the activation of enzymes, called **proteases**, which chew up proteins inside the cell. Having too much calcium can also damage the mitochondria, the energy-producers of the cell. Excessive glutamate can also allow water to enter neurons and glia, causing them to swell. Too much glutamate is not a good thing.

Cell Death: Necrosis and Apoptosis

The damage caused by excitotoxicity may ultimately lead to the death of the neurons and glia. Cell death can occur through processes called necrosis and apoptosis. **Necrosis** causes cells to swell and burst, thereby dumping their contents into the surrounding areas. In doing so, necrosis causes further damage to neighboring neurons and glial cells. During apoptosis, a program of cellular events is turned on that eventually leads to cell death. This program includes the activation of special enzymes, DNA fragmentation, and membrane degradation. Apoptosis of neurons occurs within eight hours of a spinal cord injury. An additional wave of apoptosis takes place a week later, which seems to kill glial cells selectively. Several studies in animals show that blocking apoptosis soon after the initial impact can reduce the total damage caused by a spinal cord injury. However, it is unclear how these results can be applied to humans because anti-apoptotic drugs are often very toxic and therefore cannot be administered.

NERVOUS SYSTEM REPAIR
Birth of New Neurons

The nervous system has a limited capacity for repairing itself. However, the factors that allow repair to occur successfully are still unknown. In some cases, brain or spinal cord injury can cause new neurons to be generated from stem cell precursors (see Chapter 4). Therefore, the study of stem cells is of great interest to the scientific and medical communities because of the potentially wide implications for nervous system repair. Toward this goal, scientists are looking into the possibility of using stem cell transplants as one way to promote regeneration of neurons after injuries or diseases kill them.

Regeneration of Axons: Lessons From the Spinal Cord

Much of what we know about repair of the nervous system following an injury comes from studies of the spinal cord. Although complete regeneration of axons following spinal cord injury does not occur, there is often a partial recovery of function due to the regrowth of axons. Following spinal cord injury, the damaged axons can be severed as a result of the injury or due to swelling. The region of the axon that is still connected to the target muscle completely degrades. The region of the axon that is still connected to the cell body first retracts into a ball and then begins to grow out again. Similar to what happens during development, the growing axon must accomplish several things. It has to grow out toward the target, sprout processes, and then form new synapses (see Chapter 4). But this process is much more difficult than it is during development for several reasons. For one, there are much lower levels of guidance cues and growth factors in the mature nervous system than in the developing nervous system. Furthermore, the axon has to work its way through a very dense network of neurons and glia in the mature nervous tissue in order to find the correct target. Such a dense network can be a barrier to growth. As a result, the regenerating axons sometimes overgrow or miss their targets completely. However, the fact that the axons grow again at all suggests that axons retain some growth program or that the body still produces small amounts of necessary growth factors. Therefore, scientists and doctors are currently exploring the possibility of administering extra growth factors following spinal cord injury as one way to promote axonal regrowth and functional regeneration of the nervous system after injury.

8 Diseases and Disorders

It is easy to take our good health for granted. We usually assume, for instance, that our brain works normally, that we can walk and talk properly, and that we can dream, think, and create ideas. We are able to accomplish all of these things because the neurons in our brain and spinal cord are wired properly to the rest of our body and because there is a good balance of neurotransmitters in our nervous system. However, many different things can go wrong in the nervous system to upset this balance. For example, neurodegenerative diseases can cause deterioration of the neurons in the brain and spinal cord. Imbalances in neurotransmitter levels can cause mood disorders, psychoses (conditions that distort one's reality), and other mental illnesses. Other neurological conditions cause the brain to become abnormally active, and some autoimmune diseases can cause the body to attack its own nervous system. Contrary to popular belief, diseases and disorders of the nervous system are very common. As a result, mental disorders are the third most expensive medical condition to treat in America, behind heart and lung disorders. In this chapter, you will learn about a few of these diseases and disorders and how they affect the cells of the nervous system.

NEURODEGENERATIVE DISEASES
Alzheimer's Disease: The "Tangled" Brain

One of the most common and devastating neurodegenerative diseases is **Alzheimer's disease**. It is the leading cause of **dementia**, a condition that causes a slow and progressive loss of brain function. Alzheimer's disease causes people to become disoriented and to slowly lose their high-level brain functions, such as memory, judgment skills, and reasoning abilities, until they can no longer perform normal daily activities or communicate. A person affected by Alzheimer's disease may require help getting dressed, eating, and using the restroom. In the late stages of the disease, he or she may even fail to recognize close family members and friends. The slow progression of Alzheimer's disease can last as long as 20 years. Ronald Reagan, the 40th president of the United States, lived with Alzheimer's disease for 10 years before his death on June 5, 2004. Alzheimer's disease typically affects individuals over 65 years of age, although there are cases where younger people are affected. Five to ten percent of 65-year-olds and 50% of people who are 85 years old or older will develop Alzheimer's disease. Altogether, this adds up to 4.5 million people in the United States who are living with Alzheimer's disease. Although the cause of the disease is unknown, age seems to be the main risk factor. Other risk factors include a family history of Alzheimer's disease, stroke or other brain injuries, and high cholesterol.

The devastation caused by Alzheimer's disease is a result of massive neuron death and reduced levels of the neurotransmitter acetylcholine. In particular, the brain regions affected are those that control movement, memory, and higher-level thought processes. Although the exact cause of neuronal death is unknown, researchers believe that it may be related to the presence of abnormal structures called **tangles** and **plaques** in the Alzheimer's brain (Figure 8.1). Tangles are located inside of

TANGLES

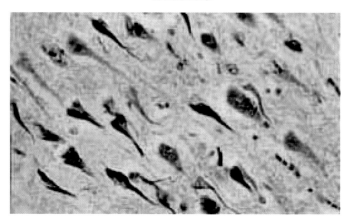

PLAQUE

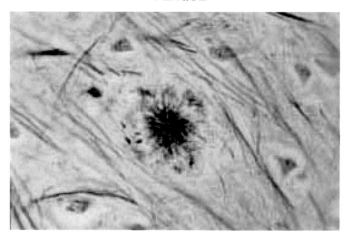

Figure 8.1 Tangles and plaques are abnormal structures found within the Alzheimer's brain. Tangles form inside neurons, while plaques occur outside.

neurons. They are made of an accumulation of proteins that form long, rope-like structures. In contrast, plaques are located outside of neurons. They are formed from the accumulation of a different protein. Although tangles and plaques can interfere with the normal communication between neurons, it is unclear

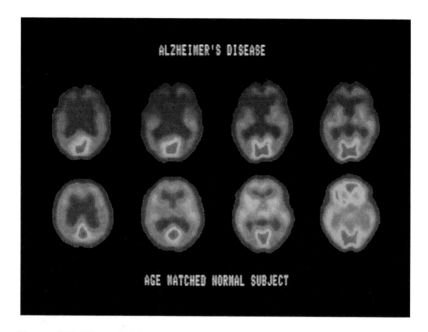

Figure 8.2 These PET scans show the brain of an Alzheimer's patient *(top)* and a healthy person of the same age *(bottom)*. Note the lower activity in the brain of the Alzheimer's patient indicated by fewer yellow and red regions.

whether these structures are the *cause* or the *result* of Alzheimer's disease. To diagnose Alzheimer's disease, doctors look for elevated levels of plaque proteins within the spinal fluid. Alternatively, they can diagnose Alzheimer's disease by looking at areas of brain shrinkage caused by neuron loss or by observing lower brain activity (Figure 8.2). Because Alzheimer's disease lowers levels of acetylcholine, the disease is often treated with medications that prevent the breakdown of this neurotransmitter. Although medication does not stop Alzheimer's disease, it can slow the progression. Currently, there is no known cure for Alzheimer's disease. However, doctors and scientists are making steady progress in understanding its causes and how to treat it.

Parkinson's Disease: A Shaky Matter

Parkinson's disease is another neurodegenerative disease that currently affects as many as 1 million Americans. This disease specifically attacks neurons within regions of the brain that control movement. As a result, someone with Parkinson's disease experiences severe trembling or shaking, loses flexibility and posture, and walks and talks more slowly. The loss of motor coordination is typically slow and gradual. However, this varies from person to person. Unlike Alzheimer's disease, Parkinson's disease normally does not affect higher-level mental processes, except in extreme cases. The tremors and muscle spasms associated with Parkinson's can often cause serious discomfort and pain. Most individuals affected with Parkinson's disease are over the age of 50. However, in rare cases, Parkinson's disease affects younger people in their 30s. Although the exact cause of Parkinson's disease is unknown, it does seem to run in families, indicating a genetic component. In support of this notion, scientific evidence has shown a link between Parkinson's disease and specific mutations of several proteins found within synapses. Environmental factors, such as pesticides, head trauma, and viruses, may pose additional risks for acquiring this disease.

Scientists have made great strides in understanding what happens in the brain of a person with Parkinson's disease. The onset of Parkinson's disease is caused by the death of a specific subset of neurons in a brain region called the **substantia nigra**, which controls several aspects of movement. These neurons of the substantia nigra use dopamine as their neurotransmitter. Therefore, when these neurons die, the dopamine levels in the brain are reduced (Figure 8.3). As a result, most treatments for Parkinson's disease focus on replenishing the lost dopamine. For example, Parkinson's patients are given medications designed to elevate dopamine levels by increasing its production, by mimicking its action, or by preventing its breakdown at

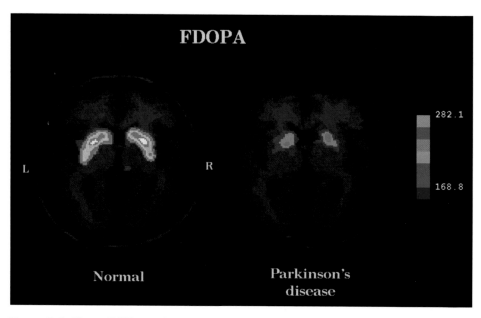

Figure 8.3 These PET scan images show the decreased levels of dopamine (*colored regions*) in a patient with Parkinson's disease as compared with a healthy person.

synapses (Figure 8.4). Such medications are usually effective in reducing the tremors and muscle spasms associated with the disease. An alternate approach is to replenish the dopamine-producing neurons themselves. This involves implanting fetal nervous tissue, which is rich in dopamine-producing neurons, into the brain of a Parkinson's patient. Although such implants have been successful at replacing the dopamine-producing neurons, this option has met with ethical, practical, and political problems due to the use of fetal tissue. In the future, doctors may be able to use stem cells to replace the dopamine neurons (for more information, see the box in Chapter 4 titled "Stem Cells"). When medications do not work, doctors may treat Parkinson's disease with deep brain stimulation or with surgery to ease some of the aggravating symptoms, such as tremors.

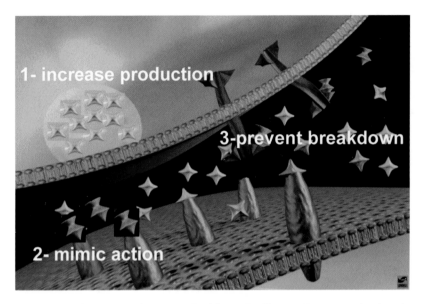

Figure 8.4 Drugs used to treat Parkinson's disease increase the levels of dopamine at the synapse by increasing its production, mimicking its action, or preventing its breakdown.

Deep brain stimulation involves using an electrode to stimulate and activate certain brain regions that regulate movement. Surgery involves drilling a hole in the skull and destroying a small part of the brain downstream of the substantia nigra. Although there is no cure for Parkinson's disease, these treatments can help the affected individual lead a more comfortable life.

Huntington's Disease: A Gene on the Scene
Huntington's disease is another progressive neurodegenerative disease that affects some 30,000 Americans. Early on, a person affected with Huntington's disease may become irritable, depressed, suspicious, or angry. As the disease progresses, he or she may lose memory, judgment, and the ability to concentrate. Eventually, the person experiences disorders of movement, including involuntary jerkiness. Difficulties with movement are due to the death of neurons in the basal ganglia, one region of the

brain that coordinates movements. Eventually, a person with Huntington's disease loses his or her ability to perform normal daily functions and requires constant care. As with the other neurodegenerative diseases, the progression of Huntington's can take anywhere between 10 and 30 years. Although the first symptoms are usually detected in adults in their 40s or 50s, there are some cases in which the symptoms first show up during adolescence.

Remarkably, Huntington's disease is caused by a dominant mutation within a single gene that holds the recipe for a protein called **huntingtin**. The fact that it is a dominant mutation means that a child who has a parent with Huntington's disease has a 50% chance of developing the disease. A simple genetic test can determine whether someone has the mutation. The Huntington's mutation results in an abnormal extension of huntingtin. Why this abnormality causes neurons to die is unknown and therefore is an active area of scientific research. There is no cure for this disease. Thus, doctors usually prescribe antidepressants and muscle-relaxing medications to help people with Huntington's disease cope with the effects this disease has on mood and movements.

MOOD DISORDERS
Major Depression

Major **depression** is a mood disorder in which someone experiences strong feelings of sadness and hopelessness. Depression is not the same as temporarily feeling down or having the blues. Instead, depression can last for several weeks, months, or even longer, if not treated properly. A person who is depressed may experience a prolonged period of diminished activity, become easily fatigued, lack an appetite, and be unable to concentrate. In general, a person who is depressed stops enjoying normal daily activities that he or she once enjoyed. Depression is a very common and costly disorder. A surprising 10% of the American population, or an estimated 20 million people, have a depressive illness. It affects children, teens, and adults alike. Although twice as many women suffer from depression as men, men are four times more likely to commit suicide as a result of being depressed. Depression may occur in repeated episodes throughout a person's lifetime. Famous people who suffered from depression include former British prime minister Winston Churchill, author Herman Melville, and poet Sylvia Plath. Risk factors for depression include a family history of depression, stress, and physical changes in the body, such as those that occur after a stroke, heart attack, or cancer.

Depression is the result of abnormally low levels of neurotransmitters in the brain. The brain pathways affected include those that use serotonin, dopamine, and norepinephrine as neurotransmitters. Thus, treatment of depression is specifically geared toward increasing the levels of these neurotransmitters. Similar to medications for Parkinson's disease, medications that successfully relieve the symptoms of depression either increase neurotransmitter production or prevent it from becoming degraded (refer back to Figure 8.4). Other medications for depression prevent the reuptake of neurotransmitters from the synaptic cleft by the transporters. The **selective serotonin reuptake inhibitors** (SSRIs) specifically prevent serotonin reuptake and, in doing so, ultimately increase the amount of serotonin available at the synapse. One example of an SSRI is the drug marketed under the trade name Prozac®. Other, newer drugs, such as Effexor® or Wellbutrin®, block the reuptake of several neurotransmitters at once. Treatment of depression with medications is usually coupled with psychological therapy or counseling. When medications do not work, there are alternative treatments such as **electroconvulsive therapy** (**ECT**). During ECT, electrodes placed on the skull deliver electrical impulses, which are designed to produce controlled, miniature seizures. Because one side effect of ECT is temporary short-term memory loss, it is rarely used.

Bipolar Disorder: Ups and Downs

Bipolar disorder is another common mood disorder in which the individual experiences periodic episodes of mania in addition to depression. A **manic episode** is characterized by prolonged levels of excessive activity, an elevated mood, insomnia, and delusions. Signs of mania include excessive talking and activity, distractibility, inflated self-esteem or grandiosity, euphoria, and increased sex drive. Bipolar disorder causes a person's mood to cycle between depressive and manic episodes, which sometimes can be accompanied by psychotic behaviors. During one particularly depressive episode, painter Vincent van Gogh cut off part of his own ear. Bipolar disorder affects some 2 million Americans, young and old. Because it runs in families, there is likely a genetic component to this disorder. In support of this, someone who has a parent with bipolar disorder is eight times more likely to develop the disorder than a person who does not.

Similar to depression, bipolar disorder is likely caused by imbalances in the levels of serotonin, norepinephrine, and dopamine. In 1948, Australian psychiatrist John Cade discovered a successful treatment for bipolar disorder. While searching for the cause of mania, he accidentally found that **lithium** had a calming effect on guinea pigs. When he gave lithium to a manic patient, it also reduced the symptoms. Later, two Danish psychiatrists discovered that lithium also prevented the recurrence of depressive episodes. Lithium is now the single best medication for the treatment of bipolar disorder. Exactly how lithium can treat both depression and mania, which are two very different behavioral states, is still unknown.

PSYCHOTIC DISORDERS
Schizophrenia

Schizophrenia is a chronic, disabling psychotic disease that causes a person to have distorted perceptions of reality (called

Figure 8.5 This drawing was done by Adolf Wolfli, an artist who had schizophrenia. Wolfli had delusions of grandeur, believing himself to be a saint.

"delusions" or "psychoses"), to experience hallucinations, and to behave in strange and often perplexing ways. For example, someone with schizophrenia may hear voices in his or her head trying to take control, or may see things that are not there. Sometimes, a person with schizophrenia may believe that he or she is being persecuted or is famous (Figure 8.5). A person with schizophrenia may also have disorganized speech patterns, strange thoughts, abnormal behaviors, and flattened emotions. Some 2 million Americans are affected by schizophrenia. The onset of this disease usually occurs in people in their mid- to late 20s (see "Mental Illness: Fact or Fiction?" box).

Mental Illness: Fact or Fiction?

"Schizophrenia is the same as having a 'split personality' like Dr. Jekyll and Mr. Hyde."

FICTION. Although the word *schizophrenia* comes from the Greek words that mean "split" and "mind," people with schizophrenia do not have multiple personalities. Multiple personality disorder is a different, rarer condition.

"Mental illnesses are medical illnesses, just like heart disease or diabetes. People with mental illnesses are not 'crazy.'"

FACT. Mental illnesses are indeed medical illnesses. They are caused by genetic and environmental factors and can usually be treated successfully with proper medical care.

"Mental illness is rare. I don't know anyone with a mental illness."

FICTION. Mental illness is surprisingly common. It can affect anyone regardless of gender, age, ethnicity, or religion. Roughly 20% of Americans experience some type of mental illness each year.

"Depression is common in teens."

FACT. Major depression affects 1 in 12 teens. It is often brought on by stress, relationship breakups, abuse, or the death of a loved one. Suicide as a result of depression is the third leading cause of teen death, after accidents and homicide. If you or someone you know is suffering from depression, seek help immediately. Additional information about teen depression is available online at

http://www.safeyouth.org/scripts/teens/depression.asp.

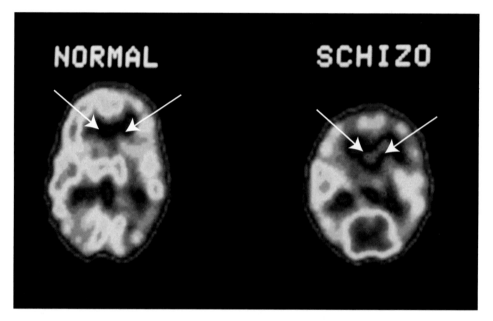

Figure 8.6 Schizophrenia causes an enlargement of the fluid-filled ventricles of the brain *(arrows)*.

Though schizophrenia affects men and women alike, men are likely to develop the condition earlier in life, in the teens or early 20s. A person with schizophrenia is not violent, but instead may seem withdrawn from social activities. There is no single cause of schizophrenia. However, because it runs in families, there appears to be a genetic component to the disease. In support of this idea, both siblings will develop schizophrenia in those cases observed in identical twins.

The brain of a person with schizophrenia has abnormally enlarged ventricles (the fluid-filled spaces in the center of the brain) (Figure 8.6). At the cellular level, schizophrenia may be caused by abnormally high levels of dopamine. Therefore, drugs that are used to treat schizophrenia are designed to block the effects of dopamine at the synapse. The drug marketed under the trade name Haldol® is a dopamine antagonist—that is, it blocks dopamine receptors. Newer drugs that have shown success treating this disease, such as Clozaril® and Risperdal®, block both dopamine and serotonin receptors. Thus, serotonin may also play a role in schizophrenia. All of these medications successfully reduce the psychotic symptoms of schizophrenia. Although there is no cure for schizophrenia, proper treatment can allow a person affected with schizophrenia to live and work comfortably within society.

NEUROLOGICAL CONDITIONS
Seizures and Epilepsy: An Overstimulated Brain

An episode in which uncontrolled electrical activity occurs in the brain is called a **seizure. Epilepsy,** a condition that makes people susceptible to seizures, was first described more than 3,000 years ago by the ancient Babylonians. The word *epilepsy* comes from the Greek word *epilambabein,* meaning "attack." A person experiencing a generalized epileptic seizure may convulse, drool, and lose consciousness. However, many seizures are virtually undetectable by an observer as they do not cause disorganized body movements. An estimated 2 million Americans of every age, race, and ethnic background experience seizures or are diagnosed with epilepsy. In fact, famous people such as the philosopher Socrates, Julius Caesar, the writer Fyodor Dostoyevsky, Napoleon Bonaparte, and Alfred Nobel—for whom the esteemed Nobel Prize was named—are said to have suffered from epilepsy. The causes of epilepsy include genetic factors, head injuries, developmental brain disorders, and poisoning.

During a seizure, neurons in the affected brain region become abnormally active and fire action potentials spontaneously (Figure 8.7). Such abnormal activity can occur anywhere in the brain and can be detected by placing electrodes on the skull or by imaging techniques. It is in this way that epilepsy is diagnosed. Epileptic brain activity may cause a massive release of glutamate, resulting in excitotoxicity that can damage neurons (see Chap-

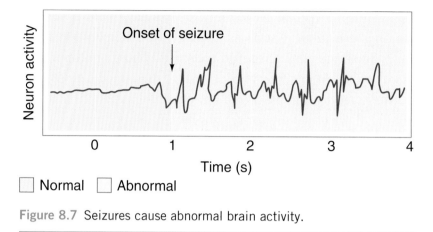

Figure 8.7 Seizures cause abnormal brain activity.

ter 7 for more details). Alternatively, abnormally low levels of the inhibitory neurotransmitter GABA can cause a seizure. By removing inhibition, the overall level of activity in the brain is increased, and therefore too little GABA can cause the same effect as too much glutamate. Medication is the most common way to treat epilepsy. Most anti-epileptic drugs work by blocking the activity of glutamate-producing neurons or by elevating GABA levels. An alternative approach involves surgical removal of the seizure area. However, this is a risky option, particularly if the area is near the language or motor centers of the brain. There is currently no cure for epilepsy. However, with proper treatment, a person with epilepsy can lead a perfectly normal life.

AUTOIMMUNE DISORDERS
Multiple Sclerosis

Multiple sclerosis (MS) is a neurological autoimmune disease that is thought to occur when the body's immune system attacks the myelin coat of its own neurons. As a result of this autoimmunity, axons become demyelinated, and nerve impulses have a hard time traveling through the nervous system.

Normally, myelin provides protection and insulation to axons, preventing the degradation of action potentials as they make their way down to the nerve terminals (see Chapter 3). However, when MS attacks the nervous system, it causes myelin to degrade. Therefore, axons lose their protective coat, and the electrical signals leak out of the axon before they reach the muscles. Thus, communication between neurons and muscles deteriorates. There is no cure for MS. However, anti-inflammatory drugs seem to reduce the pain associated with an attack.

MS usually progresses as a series of attacks. As the disease progresses, the person may experience fatigue, muscle spasms, and muscle pain. Eventually, he or she loses muscle control and becomes very weak. In half of all MS cases, a person will eventually lose his or her ability to memorize things, to concentrate, and to perform other higher-level thought processes. Multiple sclerosis affects between 200,000 and 300,000 Americans. The initial symptoms of MS usually begin between the ages of 20 and 40. Because onset occurs early in life, and because its progression is slow, MS can be a very devastating disease. For this reason, many scientists are working hard to discover what causes MS and how to prevent or treat the process of demyelination.

As recently as 50 years ago, a person who had a disease of the nervous system was sure to die. Now, with scientific discoveries and medical breakthroughs, it is possible to treat some of the symptoms associated with these disorders. Although there are no absolute cures (yet) for these diseases, scientific discovery has made it possible in some cases for a person with a disease of the nervous system to live comfortably.

■ **Learn more about brain disorders** Search the Internet for *Alzheimer's, Parkinson's, and Huntington's diseases*; *depression, bipolar disorder, schizophrenia, seizure, epilepsy*, or *multiple sclerosis*.

9 Drugs of Abuse: "High"-jacking the Synapse

Millions of Americans of all ages and races today are using and abusing drugs. Hundreds of drugs are currently classified as controlled substances, including narcotics, depressants, stimulants, hallucinogens, and marijuana. These drugs cause a wide range of effects on the body and brain, including intense feelings of pleasure, excitement, euphoria, and sensory hallucinations. When overused, drugs of abuse can also have dramatic negative effects on the heart, liver, lungs, and brain, and can even cause seizures, coma, and death. Regardless of the feelings produced by the drugs, they all have one thing in common—they cause damage to the brain by altering neurotransmitter levels at synapses. Normally, neurotransmitter levels are under a high degree of control. However, drugs of abuse swamp the pathways that control the neurotransmitter levels, often resulting in the "high" feelings that come with drug use. Many drugs of abuse are addictive because they activate the **reward pathway** in the brain (Figure 9.1). When the reward pathway is activated, the result is a feeling of pleasure and the craving associated with addiction. **Addiction** is not simply a condition of overusing drugs, but a medical condition in which the brain and the body gain a physical dependence on the drug. In this chapter, you will learn about some of the most commonly abused drugs in the United States and how they affect the cells of the nervous system.

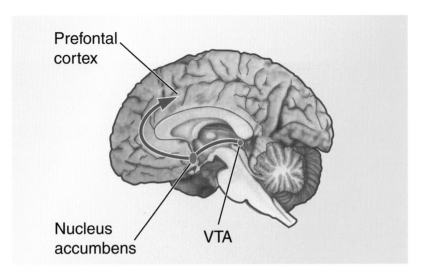

Figure 9.1 The reward pathway is connected by the VTA (ventral tegmental area), the prefrontal cortex, and the nucleus accumbens. Drugs of abuse target the reward pathway and pleasure centers of the brain.

ALCOHOL

Alcohol (ethanol) is the most widely abused legal substance among adults in the United States. Alcohol is a depressant of the central nervous system. When consumed at low levels, it causes a relaxed feeling, impairs coordination, and removes inhibitions. At higher doses, alcohol can cause slurred speech and drowsiness, change emotions, and even cause someone to pass out. Chronic abuse of alcohol can cause severe damage to the liver and brain and can lead to **alcoholism**, a condition in which a person craves alcohol or gains a physical dependence on it. Age makes a difference in whether someone becomes an alcoholic. Teens who consume large amounts of alcohol are four times more likely to become alcoholics than 21-year-olds who do the same. In extreme cases, alcohol abuse leads to Wernicke-Korsakoff syndrome, a disorder that causes a person to experience severe memory loss, to hallucinate, and to lie. In the

15-year-old male
non-drinker

15-year-old male
heavy drinker

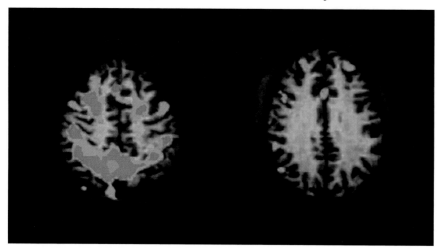

Figure 9.2 These MRI images show brain activity (*pink and red*) during a memory task. Note the lack of activity in the brain of the heavy drinker (*right*).

United States alone, 14 million people misuse or abuse alcohol. Three million of these are young Americans between the ages of 12 and 20 years, all of whom are under the legal drinking age. The three leading causes of teen death—accidents, homicides, and suicides—are all related to the consumption of alcohol. In fact, alcohol consumption contributes to the death of 1,400 college students each year. Another 500,000 students are injured as a result of alcohol-related situations.

Alcohol significantly inhibits the brain's activity (Figure 9.2). It also damages the frontal lobe and causes the fluid-filled ventricles to shrink, indicating a loss of neurons by death. Like many other drugs of abuse, alcohol can produce major effects on the cells of the nervous system because of the ease with which it crosses the blood-brain barrier (see Chapter 3). Alcohol affects many different neurotransmitter systems, including those that use norepinephrine, dopamine, serotonin, and glutamate. With a single drink, alcohol increases the production and release of dopamine in the brain pathways that deal with reward. Continued consumption of alcohol and release of dopamine eventually decreases the levels of this neurotransmitter in the brain, lowering its overall activity. Alcohol also lowers overall brain activity by reducing synaptic transmission in glutamate (excitatory) pathways and increasing it in GABA (inhibitory) pathways. Such widespread effects on the neurotransmitters somehow lead to neuronal death. Because alcohol has dramatic and devastating effects on the brain, it should be consumed cautiously. Therefore, alcohol can only be legally purchased and consumed by adults.

BARBITURATES

Barbiturates represent another class of medications that act as a depressant to the central nervous system. Barbiturates may be legally administered by a doctor to a patient before surgery to reduce anxiety or to induce relaxation. Sometimes they are used to treat insomnia and seizures. Nembutal®, Amytal®, and Luminal® are all trade names for medically administered barbiturates. On the street, barbiturates are known as sleeping pills, yellow jackets, and reds. In low doses, barbiturates cause relaxation, reduced blood pressure, and reduced heart rate. At high doses, they can overstimulate the nervous system. When barbiturates are abused, it is not uncommon for someone to overdose. In 1970, a barbiturate overdose caused the death of guitarist, singer, and songwriter Jimi Hendrix. Although the effects of barbiturates on the brain are not entirely clear, they are thought to block the formation of action potentials, thereby reducing or dampening the brain's level of activity. Because barbiturates are highly addictive, they should be used only under the supervision of a medical doctor.

COCAINE

Cocaine is a highly addictive, powerful stimulant of the central nervous system. Derived from the coca plant, cocaine comes in a variety of forms that can be inhaled (snorted), smoked, or injected. Cocaine may also be called coke, snow, and blow—all references to the powdered form of cocaine that is typically snorted. **Crack** refers to a highly purified crystalline form of cocaine that can be smoked. When taken at lower doses, cocaine causes feelings of elation, excitement, and enhanced strength that last for about an hour. At higher doses, unwanted side effects, such as paranoia, restlessness, irregular heartbeat, and hallucinations, can occur. After the initial high, the user crashes into a state of depression. The depression, combined with the desire for another high, often leads a person to take more cocaine. Thus, use of this drug comes with a high risk of becoming addicted. Death by cocaine overdose is fairly common, especially when it is combined with depressants such as alcohol. Historically, native South Americans chewed the leaves of the coca plant in order to combat fatigue. Cocaine was also used in medicinal wines in the 1880s. In fact, the original Coca-Cola® produced in 1886 contained both caffeine and cocaine and was marketed as "a valuable brain-tonic that cures all nervous afflictions." Until its removal in 1903, there were 60 milligrams (.002 ounces) of cocaine in a single, 8-ounce serving of Coca-Cola. Although cocaine has been illegal since 1914, 2 million Americans still abuse this drug (see "The Latest Facts about Teen Drug Use" box).

Cocaine targets the reward pathway and pleasure centers of the brain (recall Figure 9.1). These brain regions use dopamine as a neurotransmitter. Cocaine acts by blocking dopamine transporters at the synapse and thus preventing the reuptake of this neurotransmitter from the synaptic cleft (Figure 9.3). As a result, the levels of dopamine remain abnormally high within the synaptic cleft and all the neuronal targets receive an abnormally high level of activation. Such a high level of activity in the neurons of the reward pathway causes feelings of pleasure and craving, which underlie the addictive effects of this drug. Perhaps not surprisingly, cocaine abuse can lead to strokes, seizures, other abnormal neurological conditions, or even death.

ECSTASY

Ecstasy is a synthetic compound called MDMA, or 3,4-methylenedioxymethamphetamine. MDMA may also be called X, E, or

The Latest Facts about Teen Drug Use

Each year, the University of Michigan's Institute for Social Research performs a survey documenting the extent of drug use among 8th to 12th graders. Here are some of the interesting facts they found in 2004, as compared to 2003:

- Overall drug use of illicit drugs *decreased.*
- The number of 10th graders who used cocaine, other than crack, within the previous 30 days *increased*.
- The number of 10th graders who have ever taken Ecstasy (MDMA) *decreased*, likely because of increased perception of the dangerous risks.
- The number of 8th graders who have ever used inhalants *increased*.
- The number of 12th graders who had ever used LSD *decreased*.
- The number of 10th graders who have ever smoked a cigarette, or consumed nicotine, *decreased*. This is likely due to an increased awareness of the dangers of smoking.

Additional statistics are available online at *http://www.nida.nih.gov/Infofax/HSYouthtrends.html.*

Figure 9.3 This illustration shows the mechanism of cocaine action at the synapse. Cocaine binds to the transporters and blocks dopamine re-uptake, increasing the amount of dopamine in the synaptic cleft.

Adam. As the name implies, Ecstasy is a stimulant that causes a heightened sense of awareness and intense feelings of pleasure. These intense feelings can last anywhere from 8 to 12 hours. However, Ecstasy can also produce undesirable side effects, such as headaches, anxiety, blurred vision, and muscle cramping. In the early 1900s in Germany, the drug company Merck marketed MDMA as an appetite suppressant. Doctors used it in the 1970s as a psychotherapy tool because it helped patients communicate more clearly and gain insight into their problems. Researchers found, however, that it causes significant, long-term brain damage. Therefore, MDMA was taken off the market. Now, it is an illegal drug. More recently, Ecstasy has gained enormous popularity as a club drug taken at all-night dance parties called raves. Contrary to popular belief, it is possible to overdose on Ecstasy. Overdose can lead to panic attacks, fainting, seizures, and even death.

Ecstasy causes both short-term and long-term damage to the brain. It affects the neurons that produce the neurotransmitter serotonin. In the short term, Ecstasy increases serotonin at the synapse by stimulating its release and preventing its reuptake (similar to cocaine's effect on dopamine; see, for example, Figure 9.3). In the long term, Ecstasy depletes the brain of serotonin and specifically leads to damage of the serotonin-producing neurons. One study showed an alarming global reduction in serotonin transporters within the brains of people who abused Ecstasy, which is likely caused by the death of serotonin-producing neurons (Figure 9.4). Because Ecstasy causes degradation of the dendrites and axons of serotonin-producing neurons, these neurons and their targets become disconnected. Perhaps to compensate for this loss, the serotonin-producing neurons subsequently undergo abnormal sprouting and re-growth, which could cause them to reconnect with improper targets. Whether these effects of Ecstasy on neurons are long-term or reversible is unknown. However, a scientific study performed on monkeys showed that the brain damage caused by Ecstasy lasted well over seven years after taking the drug. The potential for long-term and perhaps permanent brain damage is one powerful reason to stay away from this drug.

HEROIN

Heroin is a highly addictive narcotic that belongs to a class of drugs called **opioids**, which also includes opium, morphine, and codeine. Opioids (or opiates) are derived from the seedpod of the opium poppy, *Papaver somniferum* (which means "the poppy that makes you sleepy"). As the name implies, opioids cause drowsiness, intense relaxation, and reduced anxiety. Perhaps this explains why the character Dorothy in the movie *The Wizard of Oz* fell into a deep sleep while walking through the poppy field. Opioids are analgesics, or painkillers. As such, they have wide medical use in hospitals. On the street, heroin is called

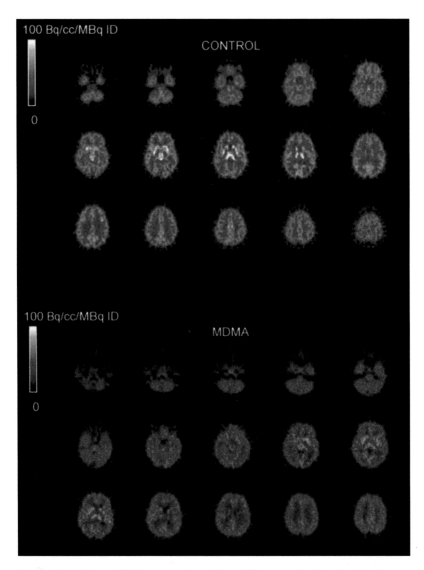

Figure 9.4 These PET scans show the difference in the level of sero-tonin transporters in the brain of an Ecstasy user and someone who does not use. Yellow and red indicate the highest level of transporter. Note the lack of transporters in the user (*bottom*) compared to the nonuser (*top*).

smack, junk, and crank. It can be injected, snorted, smoked, or taken as pills. Initially, heroin causes a rush followed by depressed breathing and clouded mental function. If used for a long time, heroin causes addiction and many other medical complications. Because the most common route for heroin delivery is through injection, its use comes with a high risk for acquiring infectious diseases, including hepatitis and HIV. Withdrawal from heroin causes severe flu-like symptoms, including chills, fever, shaking, and sweating—all of which can last up to 10 days. Recreational opioid use has been documented as far back as ancient Egypt, Greece, and Rome. Opioids were also the cause of the Opium Wars, between 1839 and 1860, in which Great Britain and China fought over trade rights. Though illegal, heroin was the fourth most common substance associated with drug-related deaths in 2002.

Within the brain are special molecules called **opioid receptors** that detect heroin and other opioids. Opioid receptors are found in the brain's reward pathway and pleasure centers. They normally respond to naturally occurring substances in the brain called **endorphins**. Endorphins are the body's natural painkillers, which get released in reaction to stress, pain, or intense exercise and can induce a euphoric, high feeling. When heroin enters the brain, it triggers a complex set of reactions at the synapses between several neurons (Figure 9.5). First, heroin binds to the opioid receptors on one neuron, activating this neuron. This activation signal is somehow communicated to a neighboring neuron, causing the neighboring neuron to release more dopamine. This increase in dopamine release ultimately overstimulates the neighboring neurons and leads to the euphoric feelings of relaxation and pleasure associated with heroin and other opiates. The repeated urge for these euphoric feelings often leads to heroin addiction.

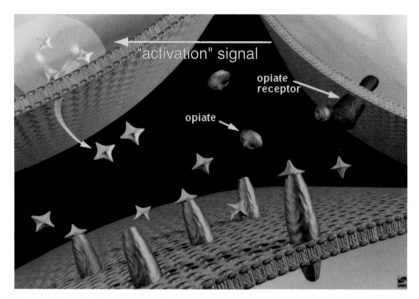

Figure 9.5 At the synapse, heroin and other opiates increase the levels of dopamine and thus activate the reward pathway.

INHALANTS

Inhalants are substances whose vapors are inhaled in order to produce a high. Inhalants include aerosols, gasoline, lighter fluid, nitrous oxide, paint thinners, glues, and many other volatile substances. When sniffed, or huffed, inhalants produce a quick high characterized by slurred speech, dizziness, and clumsy movements. Because the high is over so quickly, people often use inhalants several times per hour. A single use of inhalants can cause increased arrhythmic heart beating and sometimes lead to death by causing asphyxiation, coma, or seizures. Twenty-three million Americans have used inhalants at least once in their lives. A shocking 17% of 8th graders have used inhalants, making these drugs among the most widely abused by young people.

Prolonged use of inhalants produces major brain damage in the brain areas that control learning, movement, vision, and hearing. The damage caused by inhalants is even more extensive than that caused by cocaine. Although the effects of inhalants on the brain are not entirely clear, they do change the appearance of the white matter of the brain. Scientists believe that these changes are likely due to changes in the cellular membrane composition. However, inhalants do not appear to kill the neurons or cause demyelination of axons. Therefore, there is hope that the brain damage caused by inhalants may be reversible after a person stops using these drugs.

LSD

LSD, or lysergic acid diethylamide, is a mood altering, hallucinogenic, psychedelic drug known on the street as "acid." It comes from a fungus that grows on rye and other grains. LSD is taken orally as a pill, capsule, or on paper blotted with the drug. The effects of LSD begin 30 to 90 minutes after taking it and can last for up to 12 hours. LSD produces intense sensations and mind-altering delusions, as well as visual, auditory, and sensory hallucinations. LSD also causes increased heart rate and blood pressure, loss of appetite, and insomnia. The mind-altering experience is referred to as a "trip." Sometimes the rapid changes in sensation and the mind alterations are frightening and can cause anxiety, confusion, or panic. LSD is not addictive. However, it does produce **tolerance**, meaning that more of the drug is needed to achieve the same effect. Increased tolerance comes with a greater risk of unwanted side effects, such as severe panic or terror, which can lead to despair and death. The effects of LSD can also return even when the drug is not being used, an experience known as a **flashback**. Although the brain pathways that respond to LSD are not entirely known, it is clear that LSD binds to and activates serotonin receptors in the brain. The effects on serotonin pathways are likely to underlie the depression and schizophrenic behaviors observed in repeated LSD users. In the United States alone, 25 million people have used LSD at least once, and an estimated 500,000 people still use this drug annually.

MARIJUANA

Marijuana is one of the most widely used illegal drugs in the world. Derived from the hemp plant, *Cannabis sativa*, marijuana is also known as pot, weed, Mary Jane, and grass. Marijuana is typically smoked as a cigarette or in a pipe. At low levels, it causes one to feel relaxed or sleepy, reduces coordination, reduces the attention span, and distorts one's perception. At increased levels, marijuana can cause undesirable effects such as paranoia, hallucinations, and disorientation. The effects of marijuana usually last for three to four hours. Long-term use can affect memory, attention, and learning. In the United States alone, 18.5 million people have used marijuana, and an estimated 3 million people use it daily. Based on a 2004 survey, 6 million 8th graders use marijuana on a monthly basis.

The main active chemical in marijuana is **THC**, which stands for tetrahydrocannabinol. THC affects the hippocampus and the cerebellum, which are areas of the brain that are involved in memory and movement, respectively. Thus, these brain functions become compromised by smoking marijuana. THC binds to a special set of receptors in the brain, called **cannabinoid receptors** (Figure 9.6). Normally, cannabinoid receptors are activated by a natural compound made in the body called anandamide. When THC enters the brain, it triggers a complex set of reactions at synapses between several neurons similar to those that occur after taking heroin and other opioids. First, THC binds to the cannabinoid receptors on one neuron, thereby activating the neuron. This activation signal is somehow communicated to a neighboring neuron, causing it to release more dopamine. This increase in dopamine release ultimately over-

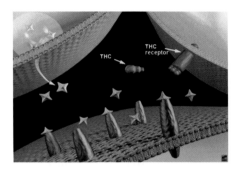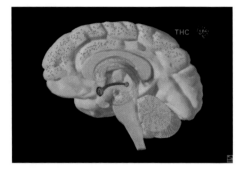

Figure 9.6 (*Left*) Marijuana is a widely abused substance. (*Right*) Marijuana's main active compound, THC (*purple*), binds to receptors found in many areas of the brain.

stimulates the neighboring neurons and leads to the euphoric feelings of relaxation and pleasure associated with smoking marijuana. Although there is some controversy surrounding the addictive nature of marijuana, it is clear that it causes serious medical problems, such as lung disorders and cancer. In some cases, for example with some cancer and HIV patients, marijuana is prescribed medically to alleviate nausea, pain, and to increase appetite. However, medical use of marijuana is very controversial.

NICOTINE

Nicotine is an addictive compound found in tobacco leaves that stimulates an increase in the heart rate and respiration. It can be smoked in cigarettes, cigars, and pipes, or it can be chewed. Tobacco use causes a variety of serious illnesses, including cancer of the lip, throat, and lungs, heart disease, and respiratory disease. Along with alcohol consumption, the use of tobacco products is one of the most critical public health problems in the United States. More than 46 million Americans smoke, and some 8 million people are living with tobacco-related illnesses. Cigarette smoking causes more than 440,000 deaths each year.

At the current rate, 6 million people currently younger than 18 will die prematurely from tobacco-related illnesses. Indeed, tobacco use is the single most avoidable cause of death in America.

Nicotine reaches the brain within 8 seconds after taking a drag on a cigarette. Because the structure of nicotine resembles that of the neurotransmitter acetylcholine, it is capable of binding to a subclass of acetylcholine receptors. Because these receptors exist in a wide range of brain areas that regulate diverse activities such as respiration, heart rate, memory, alertness, and muscle movements, the normal functioning of these processes becomes disrupted. Recent studies show that nicotine also stimulates the release of dopamine, which likely causes the rush and the feelings of pleasure associated with smoking. As with other addictive drugs, such as cocaine and heroin, dopamine release in the reward pathway probably underlies the addictive potential of nicotine. Recent scientific evidence also suggests that there are other addictive compounds in cigarette smoke. This is not surprising when one considers the fact that cigarette smoke contains more than 4,000 different chemicals.

PRESCRIPTION DRUGS

In the United States, more than 9 million people over the age of 12 use prescription drugs for recreational purposes. Commonly abused prescription drugs include Ritalin®, Adderall®, OxyContin®, and Vicodin®, among others. Ritalin and Adderall are stimulants that have effects similar to amphetamines, such as cocaine. These drugs are normally prescribed for attention-deficit/hyperactivity disorder (also known as ADHD), and in these cases have a calming effect. However, when abused, these drugs act as nervous system stimulants and are highly addictive. OxyContin and Vicodin are opioids and have a structure similar to that of heroin. These drugs are normally prescribed as painkillers after surgery or to relieve severe back pain. However, when abused, OxyContin and Vicodin activate the reward pathway of the brain and cause feelings of euphoria and drowsiness. Thus, the risks of taking these prescription drugs are similar to those of heroin, including a high potential for addiction, overdose, or death. For more details about the potential long-term effects of prescription drugs on the body and brain, see the sections in this chapter about cocaine and heroin.

Although many drugs of abuse cause addiction and disrupt the lives of the user, his or her friends, and family, there are treatments available for overcoming addiction. Successful treatments include psychotherapy, counseling, and sometimes medication. With the proper medical care, those using or abusing drugs can stop, and can return to a more normal, healthy style of living.

■ **Learn more about drug abuse and addiction** Search the Internet for *drug abuse, addiction, alcoholism,* or *prescription drug abuse.*

A FINAL WORD

As you can see, drugs of abuse have many ways of hijacking the synapse. Luckily for us, we can choose to keep our brains healthy by staying away from drugs and by making other good life choices, such as eating well and getting plenty of sleep. Hopefully, this book has helped you gain a better appreciation of the many important jobs of the neurons and glia in the brain and spinal cord. Among other things, these cells of the nervous system critically regulate our abilities to learn, remember, move, speak, and sense the world around us on a minute-by-minute basis. So, do what you can to maintain your precious brain.

Glossary

Acetylcholine Also known as ACh, it is an excitatory neurotransmitter that is used in the peripheral nervous system and causes muscle contractions. It is also used in regions of the brain that control movements and memory.

Action potential An all-or-none wave of electrical excitation that triggers the release of neurotransmitter from nerve terminals.

Active zone A special region of the nerve terminal membrane around which synaptic vesicles are clustered.

Addiction A medical condition in which the brain and the body gain a physical dependence upon a particular drug.

Adenosine triphosphate (ATP) Substance that supplies energy for many of the body's biochemical processes.

Agonists Compounds that activate receptors by mimicking neurotransmitters.

Alcoholism A condition in which a person craves alcohol or gains a physical dependence on it.

Alzheimer's disease A neurodegenerative disease that causes people to become disoriented and to slowly lose their high-level brain functions such as memory, judgment, and reasoning abilities.

Anencephaly A condition in which an embryo is formed without a cerebrum, or forebrain.

Antagonists Compounds that block neurotransmitter receptors and prevent them from responding to neurotransmitters.

Apoptosis A program of cellular events including the turning on of special enzymes, DNA fragmentation, and membrane degradation, which eventually lead to cell death.

Associational systems Systems that work between the sensory and motor systems by processing the "input" information and setting up "output" responses.

Associativity A feature of long-term synaptic plasticity, meaning that the strength of one synapse will change only if its neighbor is active at the same time.

Astrocytes   A type of glial cell in the central nervous system; they are the largest and most numerous glial cells.

Auditory cortex   Part of the brain where complex sequences of sounds such as speech and music are processed.

Auditory nerve   A collection of axons projecting from the cochlea to the brain.

Axon   A long, thin projection extending from the cell body of a neuron that transmits information very rapidly to the nerve terminals.

Barbiturates   A class of medications that act as depressants of the central nervous system.

Bipolar disorder   A mood disorder in which the individual experiences periodic episodes of mania in addition to depression.

Blood-brain barrier   A mechanism that exists at the junction between blood vessel endothelial cells and glial cells in the brain, which creates a wall separating the blood from the brain.

Brain stem   Located underneath the cerebellum and cerebral hemispheres, it is the relay station, transmitting sensory and motor information between the rest of the brain and the spinal cord.

Cannabinoid receptors   A special set of receptors in the brain to which THC, the active component of marijuana, binds.

Cell body   Also called the soma, it is the part of the neuron that houses the nucleus and other organelles. The cell body integrates all the incoming information.

Cells   The basic units of life.

Central fissure   A prominent crevice in the brain, which divides the cerebral hemispheres.

Central nervous system (CNS)   The brain and spinal cord.

Cerebellum   The part of the brain that controls many aspects of voluntary movement by helping the body both plan and coordinate complex, precise, fine movements, and maintain balance.

Cerebral hemispheres   Two symmetrical halves of the brain.

Cerebrum Also called the forebrain, it is the largest part of the human brain.

Chemical synapses Connecting points between neurons at which chemical molecules act as messengers.

Chemoattraction The process in which tropic molecules cause the growth cone to grow toward them in a positive manner.

Chemorepulsion The process in which tropic molecules cause the growth cone to grow away from them in a negative manner.

Cilia Special thin, hair-like extensions on the upper surface of hair cells.

Closed head injury A traumatic brain injury in which the damage is kept confined within the skull.

Cocaine A highly addictive, powerful stimulant of the central nervous system, derived from the coca plant.

Cochlea Part of the inner ear that houses the hair cells.

Color blindness The result of a genetic defect in photopigment production, which causes an inability to distinguish red from green.

Concussion A type of closed head injury that often results in bruising of the brain and temporary impairment of brain function.

Cones A type of photoreceptor, they are sensitive to bright light and color and are most active during daytime vision.

Cornea A clear tissue on the front surface of the eye through which light enters.

Crack A highly purified crystalline form of cocaine that can be smoked.

Dementia A condition that causes a slow and progressive loss of brain function.

Demyelination A process through which axons lose their insulating myelin coat.

Dendrites Small projections that extend from the cell body of a neuron like tree branches.

Deoxyribonucleic acid (DNA) String of molecules that carry the genetic information necessary for the organization and functioning of most living cells and that control the inheritance of characteristics.

Depression A mood disorder in which someone experiences strong feelings of sadness and hopelessness.

Dopamine Excitatory neurotransmitter that is involved in motivation and reward.

Echolocation The sonar-like ability used by bats, dolphins, and other animals to detect objects, including prey.

Ecstasy (MDMA) An illegal drug of abuse that causes a heightened sense of awareness and intense feelings of pleasure.

Ectoderm The outer layer of cells in a developing embryo from which the nervous system is constructed.

Electrical synapses Synapses at which electrical impulses serve as the messenger.

Electroconvulsive therapy (ECT) An alternative treatment for depression in which electrodes placed on the skull deliver electrical impulses, to produce miniature seizures.

Endoplasmic reticulum (ER) A complex network of membranes extending from the nucleus that helps the cell synthesize proteins.

Endorphins The body's natural painkillers, which get released in reaction to stress, pain, or intense exercise and can induce a euphoric "high" feeling.

Epilepsy A condition that makes people susceptible to seizures.

Excitatory Referring to neurotransmitters that "excite," or increase the activity of the neurons that detect them.

Excitotoxicity A harmful effect on neurons caused by overstimulating neurons, which is due to having an excess of the neurotransmitter glutamate at the synapse.

Facilitation A type of short-term synaptic plasticity, it is an enhancement of neurotransmitter release that occurs when more than one action potential reaches the nerve terminal within a short period of time.

Filopodia   Small finger-like projections that help the growth cone of an axon find its way to the target.

Flashback   An experience in which the effects of LSD can return even when the drug is not being used.

Forebrain   Another name for the cerebrum.

Fracture   A type of traumatic brain injury that occurs when an object physically breaks the skull. These injuries can cause major and permanent brain damage.

Frontal lobe   The front part of the brain that is involved in reasoning, planning, organization, emotions, problem-solving, and working memory.

GABA   The major inhibitory neurotransmitter, whose letters stand for gamma-aminobutyric acid.

Ganglia   Small sacks that lie along both sides, but outside, of the spinal cord.

Gastrulation   The process through which a developing embryo undergoes an elaborate series of infoldings that generate three layers of cells called the ectoderm, mesoderm, and endoderm.

Glia   The other major class of cells in the nervous system, besides neurons, with a variety of functions that include neuronal support, nutrition, insulation, and activity.

Glomerulus   The functional unit of the olfactory bulb in the brain; it is a small group of neurons that receives input from a subset of neurons in the nose that contain the same type of receptor.

Glutamate   The major excitatory neurotransmitter, used by more than half of the synapses in the brain and spinal cord.

Golgi apparatus   An organelle found in eukaryotic cells that processes proteins and sorts them into secretory vesicles. It functions as a central delivery system for the cell.

Gray matter   Named for its dull grayish color, it is the layer of the nervous system comprising dendrites, cell bodies, and nerve terminals.

Growth cone   A highly motile structure found at the end of growing axons that is constantly extending and retracting in order to find the target.

Hair cells   Neurons within the cochlea that are sensitive to the frequency of sound vibrations and that convert these mechanical vibrations into action potentials.

Heroin   A highly addictive narcotic that belongs to a class of drugs called opioids and that causes drowsiness and intense relaxation and reduces anxiety.

Huntingtin   The protein that is mutated in Huntington's disease.

Huntington's disease   A progressive, inherited, neurodegenerative disease that causes irritability, depression, and anger in addition to loss of memory, judgment, and concentration.

Inhalants   Substances that are inhaled to achieve a high.

Inhibitory   Referring to neurotransmitters that "inhibit," or decrease the activity of the neurons that detect them.

Iris   A flattened ring of pigmented tissue containing bundles of smooth muscle to contract and dilate the pupil. It forms the colored portion of the eye.

Lateral geniculate nucleus   A region deep within the forebrain in which the retinal inputs from the right eye and left eye are separated into distinct layers.

Lens   The part of the eye that focuses the light onto the retina.

Lithium   A medication that is regularly used to treat bipolar disorder.

Long-term depression (LTD)   The process that occurs when repeated synaptic activity causes a long-lasting decrease in the response of a neuron.

Long-term potentiation (LTP)   The process that occurs when repeated synaptic activity causes a long-lasting increase in the response of a neuron.

LSD   Lysergic acid diethylamide; it is a mood-changing, hallucinogenic, psychedelic drug known on the street as "acid."

Macular degeneration   A condition in which photoreceptors die, causing a loss of vision.

Manic episode   A period characterized by an elevated mood and excessive activity and which cycles with depressive episodes in a person with bipolar disorder.

Marijuana   One of the most widely used illegal drugs in the world, it causes relaxation and sleepiness, reduces coordination, reduces the attention span, and distorts one's perception when it is smoked or ingested.

Microglia   The smallest of all glial cells in the nervous system. Microglia serve as the immune system for the nervous system by rapidly destroying invading microbes or removing dead cells in the brain and spinal cord.

Mitochondria   Organelles that produce ATP and provide energy to a cell.

Motor neuron   A neuron that has the specific function of driving muscle contraction.

Motor systems   Parts of the nervous system that respond to the information taken in by the sensory systems. They are the "output" systems in the body that control voluntary skeletal muscle movements.

Multiple sclerosis (MS)   A neurological disease that causes axons to lose their insulating myelin coat via a process called demyelination.

Myelin   Fatty substance found in the wrapping of axons that gives the white matter of the brain its color. The role played by myelin is similar to that of insulation on an electrical wire.

Necrosis   A process that kills cells by causing them to swell and burst.

Nerve growth factor (NGF)   A trophic molecule that is essential in the development and survival of neurons in both the central and peripheral nervous systems.

Nerve terminals   The endings on axons from which neurotransmitters are released.

Nervous system   The major system of control, regulation, and communication in the body, which consists of the brain, spinal cord, and complex networks of nerves that connect the brain and spinal cord to all parts of the body.

Neural crest cell   A type of precursor cell in the developing nervous system that has the potential to become either a neuron or a glial cell.

Neural groove   A thick infolding of the ectoderm that is formed during the early stages of nervous system development.

Neural stem cells   A type of precursor cell in the developing nervous system that produces more precursor cells.

Neural tube   A hollow cylinder of cells in a developing embryo, from which the brain and spinal cord will develop.

Neurite   A long, thin membrane projection that will eventually become a dendrite or an axon of a neuron.

Neuroblast   A type of precursor cell in the developing nervous system that is nondividing and that eventually gives rise to a neuron.

Neurogenesis   "Birth of neurons," which occurs from the neural tube.

Neuromuscular junctions   Chemical synapses between peripheral neurons and muscles.

Neurons   Individual nerve cells.

Neurotransmitters   Chemicals that convey or inhibit nerve impulses at a synapse.

Neurotransmitter transporters   Molecules that shuttle neurotransmitters from the synaptic cleft back into the nerve terminal where they can be repackaged in synaptic vesicles.

Neurulation   Process in the development of an embryo during which the neural tube is formed.

Neutrophils   The cells that are the first to respond to an injury during the immune response.

Norepinephrine   A neurotransmitter that is a derivative of dopamine and that helps to regulate the "fight or flight" response to stress.

Nucleus   An organelle that houses the genetic material of the cell, deoxyribonucleic acid (DNA).

Occipital lobe   Region at the back of the brain that processes many features of visual information.

Odorant   Airborne molecule detected by the nose; many odorants produce a smell.

Odorant receptors   Molecules found on the surface of olfactory receptor neurons that bind to and detect specific odorants.

Olfactory bulb   A region of the forebrain that receives input from the neurons of the olfactory epithelium.

Olfactory cortex   The part of the brain that processes odor signals.

Olfactory epithelium   A sheet of cells within the nasal cavity made of olfactory receptor neurons and their supporting cells.

Olfactory receptor neuron   Neurons found in the olfactory epithelium that contain odorant receptors on their surface.

Oligodendrocytes   A type of glial cell in the central nervous system that produces a fatty substance called myelin, which wraps around axons in layers and insulates them.

Opioid receptors   Molecules that bind to and detect heroin and other opioids. They are found in the brain's reward pathway and pleasure centers.

Opioids   A class of drugs, which includes opium, morphine, and codeine. Opioids are all derived from the seedpod of the opium poppy.

Optic nerve   A collection of axons arising from neurons in the retina.

Organelles   Small, internal compartments contained within cells, including neurons.

Ossicles   The small bones of the middle ear.

Parietal lobe   Located behind the frontal lobe of the brain, it processes sensory information from the environment.

Parkinson's disease   A neurodegenerative disease characterized by muscle spasms and tremors that specifically attacks neurons within regions of the brain that control movement.

Peripheral nervous system (PNS)   An elaborate network of nerves that reaches out to all parts of the body.

Phagocytose   To "chew up" or "eat" cells.

Phantom limb   Also called phantom pain, it's a phenomenon experienced by amputees in which a sensation of tingling, burning, or pain is perceived where the missing limb or digit used to be.

Photopigments   Light-sensitive molecules.

Photoreceptors   Neurons that detect photons (particles) of light.

Plaques   Accumulations of proteins found outside of neurons and that characterize Alzheimer's brains.

Plasma membrane   A thin two-layer sheet made of lipid molecules and proteins, which surrounds all cells, including neurons.

Postsynaptic   Referring to the "receiving" side of the synapse, which can be a dendrite, cell body, axon, or nerve terminal.

Post-tetanic potentiation   A type of short-term synaptic plasticity in which the nerve terminal retains its ability to release more neurotransmitters for up to several minutes.

Presynaptic   Referring to the "sending" side of the synapse, which is usually a nerve terminal.

Proteases   Enzymes that chew up proteins inside a cell.

Proteins   Polymers of amino acids strung together, which are required for the structure, function, and regulation of all cells in the body.

Pupil   The contractile aperture in the iris of the eye.

Radial glial cells   Cells used by neuroblasts as a physical guidance cue to their final destination.

Retina   Thin layer of tissue at the back of the eye that contains photoreceptor neurons.

Retinotopic (visual) map   The orderly representation of visual space that begins in the retina and continues to the brain.

Reward pathway   A pathway in the brain involving the ventral tegmental area that is activated by a rewarding stimulus.

Rods   A type of photoreceptor, they are sensitive in dim light and insensitive to color. Rods are most active during night vision.

Schizophrenia   A chronic, disabling psychotic disease that causes a person to have distorted perceptions of reality (delusions or psychoses), to experience hallucinations, and to behave in strange and often perplexing ways.

Schwann cells A type of glial cell in the peripheral nervous system that produces a fatty substance called myelin, which wraps around axons in layers and insulates them.

Secretory vesicles Small, membrane-bound organelles that are derived from the Golgi apparatus and that contain material to be released at the cell surface.

Seizure An episode in which the brain is overactivated.

Selective serotonin reuptake inhibitors (SSRIs) A class of medications used for the treatment of depression that work by preventing the reuptake of serotonin at the synapse.

Sensory neuron A type of neuron found in the peripheral nervous system that detects heat, pain, and stretch through receptors on the skin, and sends information to the spinal cord.

Sensory systems Parts of the nervous system that acquire and process information about the environment. They are the "input" systems in the body, including those that process information about the five senses: sight, sound, taste, smell, and touch.

Serotonin Excitatory neurotransmitter that regulates sleep, wakefulness, states of alertness, and emotions.

Somatosensory cortex A region of the forebrain that interprets information about touch to the skin.

Somatosensory receptors Molecules found on the cell surface of a sensory neuron that detects information about touch to the skin.

Somatotopic map An orderly representation of the body's surface found in the responses of neurons in the somatosensory cortex.

Spina bifida A condition caused by failure of the neural tube to seal during development.

Spinal cord Major part of the central nervous system, which begins at the base of the brain stem and runs the entire length of the upper body, sending out nerves that connect to skeletal muscles all over the body.

Spine A structure found along the length of a dendrite, which undergoes structural and functional synaptic plasticity.

Stem cells   Undifferentiated cells that have the potential to develop into any kind of cell in the body.

Stroke   A condition in which a blood clot blocks an artery and prevents oxygen from reaching the brain, or in which a brain hemorrhage occurs.

Substantia nigra   The brain region that controls several aspects of movements; in Parkinson's disease, the neurons of this region selectively die.

Subventricular zone   An area of the adult forebrain that retains neural stem cells.

Synapse   The point at which neurons connect.

Synapse elimination   During development, the process of axons retracting and disconnecting all of their synapses due to losing the synaptic competition.

Synapse specificity   A feature of synaptic plasticity meaning that only the active synapses undergo a change in strength, while the inactive synapses remain unchanged.

Synaptic cleft   A very small gap between the presynaptic and postsynaptic side of a synapse.

Synaptic depression   A type of short-term synaptic plasticity in which the nerve terminal becomes overwhelmed and cannot efficiently recycle synaptic vesicles, resulting in a decrease of neurotransmitter release.

Synaptic plasticity   Activity-dependent changes in synapse structure and function.

Synaptic transmission   The process through which neurons at chemical synapses communicate with each other.

Synaptic vesicles   Secretory vesicles found in the nerve terminal that contain neurotransmitter molecules.

Tangles   Accumulations of proteins found inside of neurons and that characterize Alzheimer's brains.

Tastants   Ingested molecules.

Taste cells   Special neurons located within taste buds that contain taste receptors.

Taste receptors   Molecules located on the surface of taste cells that detect tastants and transmit information about whether they are salty, sour, sweet, bitter, or savory.

T cell   A type of immune cell that can attack and eliminate cells infected by pathogens.

Temporal lobe   Part of the brain located below the parietal lobe and the lateral fissure. It is mainly concerned with processing auditory (hearing) information.

THC   The main active chemical in marijuana, the letters stand for delta 9-tetrahydrocannabinol.

Tolerance   A condition in which more of a drug is needed to achieve the same effect it once had.

Tonotopic (tone) map   The orderly representation of sound frequencies that begins in the organization of hair cells within the cochlea and that is retained all the way to the brain.

Transient ischemic attack (TIA)   A mini-stroke, which often has only temporary effects on brain function and which is often complete within five minutes.

Trophic molecules   Often produced by the target, these are molecules that support the survival and growth of the axons once the target has been reached.

Tropic molecules   Molecules that physically guide the growth cones of axons.

Tympanic membrane   Also known as the eardrum, it functions in the mechanical reception of sound waves and in their transmission to the site of sensory reception.

Visual cortex   A region of the occipital lobe, which interprets information about the orientation and color of visual images.

White matter   The layer of the nervous system made of axons and their myelin coating, which has a white color.

Bibliography

Barondes, S. *Molecules and Mental Illness.* New York: Scientific American Library, 1993.

Diamond, M. C., A. B. Scheibel, G. M. Murphy, and T. Harvey. "On the Brain of a Scientist: Albert Einstein." *Experimental Neurology* 88 (1985): 198–204.

Fields, R. D. "The Other Half of the Brain." *Scientific American* 290 (2004): 55–61.

Fields, R. D., and B. Stevens-Graham. "New Insights into Neuron-Glia Communication." *Science* 298 (2002): 556–562.

Kandel, E. R., J. H. Schwartz, and T. M. Jessell. *Principles of Neural Science*, 4th ed. New York: McGraw-Hill, 2000.

McCann, U. D., U. Scheffel, R. F. Dannals, and G. A. Ricaurte. "Positron Emission Tomographic Evidence of Toxic Effects of MDMA ("Ecstasy") on Brain Serotonin Neurons in Human Beings." *Lancet* 352 (1998): 1433–1437.

McNamara, J. O. *Neuroscience,* 3rd ed. Sunderland, MA: Sinauer Associates, Inc. Publishers, 1997.

Purves, D., G. J. Augustine, D. Fitzpatrick, L. C. Katz, A. S. LaMantia, and J. O. McNamara. *Neuroscience,* 3rd ed. Sunderland, MA: Sinauer Associates, Inc. Publishers, 2004.

Streit, W. J., and C. A. Kincaid-Colton. "The Brain's Immune System." *Scientific American* 273 (1995): 54–61.

Ullian, E. M., S. K. Sapperstein, K. S. Christopherson, and B. A. Barres. "Control of Synapse Number by Glia." *Science* 291 (2001): 657–661.

Further Reading

Ackerman, D. *A Natural History of the Senses.* New York: Vintage, 1991.

Restak, R. *Mysteries of the Mind.* Washington, DC: National Geographic, 2001.

———. *The Secret Life of the Brain.* New York: Joseph Henry Press, 2001.

Sanes, D. H., T. A. Reh, and W. A. Harris, eds. *Development of the Nervous System.* New York: Academic Press, 2000.

Taussig, M. *The Nervous System.* New York: Routledge, 1991.

Websites

Alzheimer's Organization. "What Is Alzheimer's Disease?" 2005. Available online at *http://www.alz.org/AboutAD/WhatIsAD.asp.*

Centers for Disease Control and Prevention. "Chronic Disease Prevention. Targeting Tobacco Use: The Nation's Leading Cause of Death." August 10, 2004. Available online at *http://www.cdc.gov/nccdphp/aag/aag_osh.htm.*

Christopher Reeve Homepage. "Biography of Christopher Reeve: September 25, 1952–October 10, 2004." Available online at *http://www.chrisreevehomepage.com/biography.html.*

Cleveland Clinic Health Information Center. "Traumatic Brain Injury." Available online at *http://www.clevelandclinic.org/health/health-info/docs/2000/2095.asp?index58874.*

Epilepsy Foundation. "What Is Epilepsy?" Available online at *http://www.epilepsyfoundation.org/answerplace/About-Epilepsy.cfm.*

Kid's Health. "Alzheimer's Disease." Available online at *http://www.kidshealth.org/kid/grownup/conditions/alzheimers.html.*

Michael J. Fox Foundation for Parkinson's Research. "About Parkinson's." Available online at *http://www.michaeljfox.org/parkinsons/index.php.*

National Institute of Mental Health. "Bipolar Disorder." April 9, 2004. Available online at *http://www.nimh.nih.gov/publicat/bipolar.cfm.*

———. "Teenage Brain: A Work in Progress." 2001. Available online at *http://www.nimh.nih.gov/publicat/teenbrain.cfm.*

National Institute of Neurological Disorders and Stroke. "Seizures and Epilepsy: Hope Through Research." January 6, 2005. Available online at *http://www.ninds.nih.gov/disorders/epilepsy/detail_epilepsy.htmAWhat%20is%20Epilepsy.*

———. "Spinal Cord Injury: Emerging Concepts." September 23, 2004. Available online at *http://www.ninds.nih.gov/news_and_events/proceedings/sci_report.htmAAnatomical.*

———. "Stroke Information." Available online at *http://www.ninds.nih.gov/disorders/stroke/stroke.htm.*

———. "Transient Ischemic Attack Information." Available online at *http://www.ninds.nih.gov/disorders/tia/tia.htm.*

————. "Traumatic Brain Injury Information." Available online at *http://www.ninds.nih.gov/disorders/tbi/tbi.htm.*

National Institute on Alcohol Abuse and Alcoholism. "Alcohol's Damaging Effects on the Brain." October 2004. Available online at *http://www.niaaa.nih.gov/publications/aa63/aa63.htm.*

National Institute on Drug Abuse. "The Brain & the Actions of Cocaine, Opiates, and Marijuana." Ocober 4, 2002. Available online at *http://www.nida.nih.gov/pubs/teaching/Teaching5.html.*

————. "Inhalants." December 7, 2004. Available online at *http://www.drugabuse.gov/drugpages/inhalants.html.*

National Institute on Drug Abuse for Teens. "The Science Behind Drug Abuse. Nicotine." Available online at *http://teens .drugabuse.gov/facts/facts_nicotine2.aspAtop.*

National Institutes of Health. "Stem Cell Information." Available online at *http://stemcells.nih.gov/info/basics/basics1.asp.*

National Youth Violence Prevention Resource Center. "Depression." Available online at *http://www.safeyouth.org/scripts/teens/ depression.asp.*

Neuroscience for Kids. Available online at *http://faculty.washington .edu/chudler/neurok.html.*

————. "Alcohol." Available online at *http://faculty.washington .edu/chudler/alco.html.*

Neurosurgery On-Call. Available online at *http://www.neurosurgery .org/cybermuseum/pre20th/epapyrus.html.*

Nobel prize.org. Available online at *http://www.nobelprize.org.*

————. "Rita Levi-Montalcini Autobiography." Available online at *http://nobelprize.org/medicine/laureates/1986/levi-montalcini- autobio.html.*

Parents: The Anti-Drug. "Drug Information." Available online at *http://www.theantidrug.com/drug_info/.*

Parkinson's Disease Foundation. Available online at *http://www .pdf.org/.*

"Phineas Gage's Story." Available online at *http://www.deakin .edu.au/hbs/GAGEPAGE/Pgstory.htm.*

Scheibel, A. B. "Embryonic Development of the Human Brain." Available online at *http://www.newhorizons.org/neuro/scheibel.htm.*

Society for Neuroscience. "Brain Briefings. Young Brains on Alcohol." 2004. Available online at *http://web.sfn.org/content/Publications/ BrainBriefings/brain_on_alcohol.html.*

Spina Bifida Association of America. Available online at *http://www.sbaa.org/site/PageServer?pagename5index.*

Synapse Web, Medical College of Georgia. Available online at *http://www.synapses.mcg.edu.*

Index

■ About the Authors

Jennifer Morgan is originally from Rutherfordton, North Carolina. She graduated in 1991 with highest honors from RS Central High School. From there, she went to the University of North Carolina at Chapel Hill. She began studying neurobiology during her sophomore year under the guidance of Dr. Ann Stuart. In 1995, she graduated with a B. S. degree with honors in Biology. After taking a year off to continue her research, Morgan began her graduate training at Duke University under the guidance of Dr. George Augustine. She earned a Ph.D. in Neurobiology in 2001. Morgan continues her training as a post-doctoral fellow in the laboratory of Dr. Pietro De Camilli at Yale University, where she currently studies synaptic vesicle recycling. Her research has been supported by a Brown-Coxe Postdoctoral Fellowship (Yale), a Grass Fellowship in Neurosciences (Grass Foundation/MBL), and an individual postdoctoral National Research Service Award (NIH/NIMH). Throughout her career as a scientist, Morgan has spent many summers doing research and teaching at the Marine Biological Laboratory (MBL) in Woods Hole, Massachusetts. In 2004, she was elected a member of the MBL Corporation. When she is not working, Morgan enjoys singing and playing bass guitar in her band called "The Secret Ink," traveling, and teaching her two cats to do tricks.

Ona Bloom is postdoctoral fellow at the Yale University School of Medicine. She has been interested in the interface between the nervous and immune systems since her senior year at Barnard College. She graduated with a B.A. degree in history from Barnard College in 1992 and began working as a research assistant under the supervision of Dr. Kevin J. Tracey, where she participated in his studies on the interactions between the immune and nervous systems. In 2001, Bloom earned her Ph.D. from the Rockefeller University in New York

City, under the supervision of Nobel laureate Paul Greengard. Her doctoral work concentrated on the molecular anatomy of neuronal synapses. Bloom is currently continuing her training at the Yale University School of Medicine under the supervision of Professor Ira Mellman in the departments of Cell Biology and Immunology. Bloom's fellowship has been funded by the National Institutes of Health and by the Cancer Research Institute. Currently, her scientific work focuses on the role of neuronal proteins at the immunological synapse, which is the place where antigen-presenting cells communicate with lymphocytes. In the future, Bloom plans to continue working at the interface of the nervous and immune systems. When not at work, Bloom enjoys cooking, theater, music, and travel.

■ Picture Credits

Katz, A. S. LaMantia, and J. O. McNamara. *Neuroscience*. 3rd edition. Sunderland, MA: Sinauer Associates, Inc. Publishers, 2004.

56: Greg Gambino / 20•64 Design
57: (A) McGraw-Hill Encyclopedia of Science and Technology Online
57: (B) Kristen Harris / Synapse Web
57: (C) Menahem Segal and Edi Korkotian / Weizmann Institute
58: Greg Gambino / 20•64 Design
60: Florian Engert / Harvard University
63: Greg Gambino / 20•64 Design
66: Greg Gambino / 20•64 Design
67: (A) ©Peter Lamb
67: (B) and (C) Greg Gambino / 20•64 Design
70: Greg Gambino / 20•64 Design
72: Greg Gambino / 20•64 Design
73: Greg Gambino / 20•64 Design
77: Greg Gambino / 20•64 Design
79: National Institutes of Health
80: Dana Fineman and the Christopher Reeve Paralysis Foundation
82: CNRI / Science Photo Library
90: Simon Lovestone
91: ©Roger Regsmeyer / CORBIS
93: McGill University
94: National Institute on Drug Abuse
98: Wikipedia
100: ©John D. Cunningham / Visuals Unlimited
102: Greg Gambino / 20•64 Design; Adapted from Purves, D. G., J. Augustine, D. Fitzpatrick, L. C. Katz, A. S. LaMantia, and J. O. McNamara. *Neuroscience*. 3rd edition. Sunderland, MA: Sinauer Associates, Inc. Publishers, 2004.
105: Greg Gambino / 20•64 Design
106: Society for Neuroscience
110: National Institute on Drug Abuse
112: The Lancet
114: National Institute on Drug Abuse
117: (left) National Institute on Drug Abuse
117: (right) National Institute on Drug Abuse